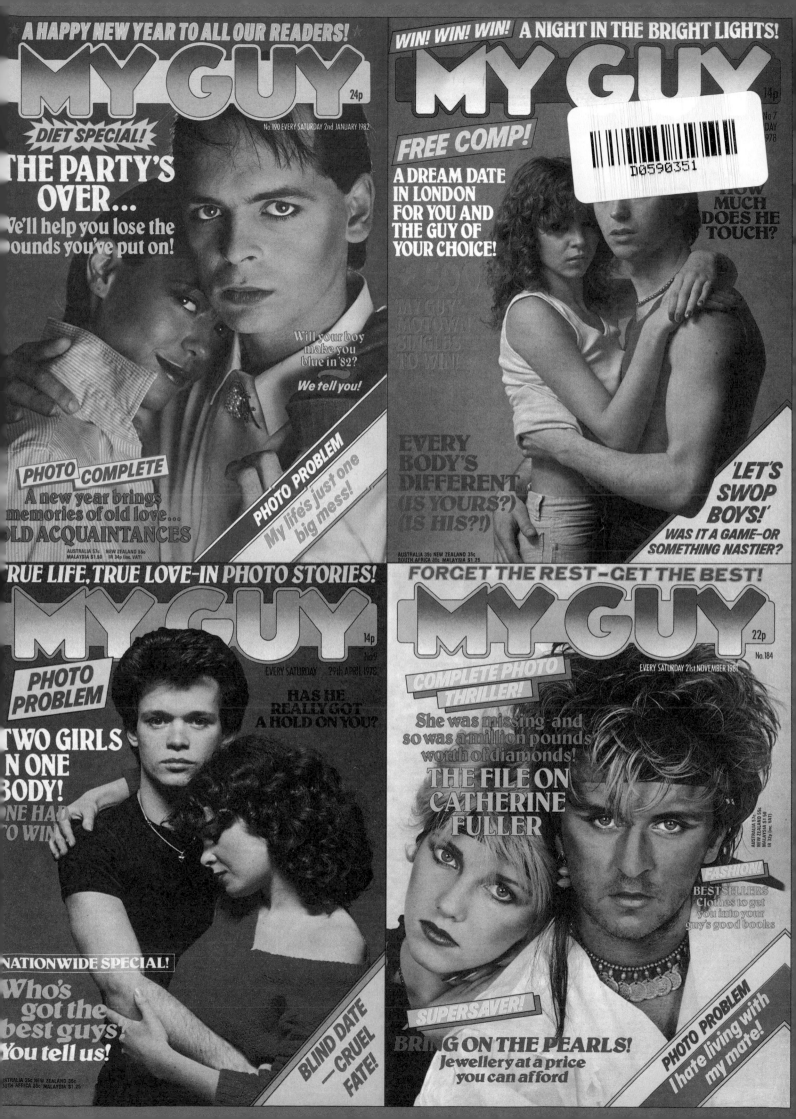

Top left cover:

A HAPPY NEW YEAR TO ALL OUR READERS!

MY GUY

24p

DIET SPECIAL!

No.190 EVERY SATURDAY 2nd JANUARY 1982

THE PARTY'S OVER...

We'll help you lose the pounds you've put on!

Will your boy make you blue in '82?

We tell you!

PHOTO COMPLETE

A new year brings memories of old love...
OLD ACQUAINTANCES

PHOTO PROBLEM
My life's just one big mess!

AUSTRALIA 57c NEW ZEALAND 55c
MALAYSIA $1.50 IR 34p (inc. VAT)

Top right cover:

WIN! WIN! WIN! A NIGHT IN THE BRIGHT LIGHTS!

MY GUY

14p

No.7
DAY
1978

FREE COMP!

A DREAM DATE IN LONDON FOR YOU AND THE GUY OF YOUR CHOICE!

HOW MUCH DOES HE TOUCH?

'MY GUY' MOTOWN SINGLES TO WIN!

EVERY BODY'S DIFFERENT (IS YOURS?) (IS HIS?!)

'LET'S SWOP BOYS!'
WAS IT A GAME—OR SOMETHING NASTIER?

AUSTRALIA 35c NEW ZEALAND 35c
SOUTH AFRICA 35c MALAYSIA $1.25

Bottom left cover:

TRUE LIFE, TRUE LOVE-IN PHOTO STORIES!

MY GUY

14p

No.9
EVERY SATURDAY 29th APRIL 1978

PHOTO PROBLEM

HAS HE REALLY GOT A HOLD ON YOU?

TWO GIRLS IN ONE BODY!
ONE HAD TO WIN!

NATIONWIDE SPECIAL!

Who's got the best guys?
You tell us!

BLIND DATE —CRUEL FATE!

AUSTRALIA 35c NEW ZEALAND 35c
SOUTH AFRICA 35c MALAYSIA $1.25

Bottom right cover:

FORGET THE REST—GET THE BEST!

MY GUY

22p

No.184
EVERY SATURDAY 21st NOVEMBER 1981

COMPLETE PHOTO THRILLER!

She was missing and so was a million pounds worth of diamonds!

THE FILE ON CATHERINE FULLER

AUSTRALIA 57c NEW ZEALAND 55c
MALAYSIA $1.50 IR 22p (inc. VAT)

FASHION!
BESTSELLERS
Clothes to get you into your guy's good books

SUPERSAVER!

BRING ON THE PEARLS!
Jewellery at a price you can afford

PHOTO PROBLEM
I hate living with my mate!

D0590351

The Best of

VOLUME 1

Top left cover:

TRUE LIFE, TRUE LOVE—REAL PHOTO STORIES!

MY GUY

16p

No. 26
EVERY SATURDAY
26th AUGUST 1978

5 PAGE PHOTO STORY

IF I CAN'T HAVE YOU...
No-one else will!

IS HE MORE THAN A MATE?

STAR GUY

NAUGHTY NICHOLAS!
The guy with too much twinkle!

PHOTO PROBLEM
BOYS ARE JUST A BLUR TO ME!

AUSTRALIA 35c NEW ZEALAND 35c
SOUTH AFRICA 35c
MALAYSIA $1.25

Top right cover:

FORGET THE REST—PLAY THE BEST!

MY GUY

24p

No. 199 EVERY SATURDAY 6th MARCH 1982

FREE!

This Beautiful Bracelet!

STARTS TODAY!
How your food affects your figure, face and moods!

INSIDE –
MY GUY BINGO!

NO PRIZES! NO CASH!
—but lots of fun and the toughest psycho test you've ever taken!

Will you still need them...
WHEN THEY'RE 64?
See Adam as an old man!

AUSTRALIA 57c NEW ZEALAND 55c
MALAYSIA $1.50 IR 34p (inc. VAT)

Bottom left cover:

INSIDE!

£25 IF YOU SPOT YOUR GUY!

MY GUY

14p

No. 8
EVERY SATURDAY
22nd APRIL 1978

WE'VE SNAPPED FELLAS—IN SECRET!

PICK YOURS OUT—AND CLAIM A PRIZE!

WILL YOU ONLY LOVE ONCE?

PROBLEM PHOTOS
SHAMED—BY THE CLOTHES SHE WORE!

NEW PHOTO STORY: WHEN DREAMS TURN TO SCREAMS...!

AUSTRALIA 35c NEW ZEALAND 35c
SOUTH AFRICA 35c MALAYSIA 1.25

Bottom right cover:

★★★★★ WE'RE 200 TODAY! ★★★★★

MY GUY

24p

EVERY SATURDAY 13th MARCH 1982 No. 200

PHOTO COMPLETE

She turned the pages of her past to find a love she'd lost
MEMORIES OF MY GUY

INSIDE
PHOTO STORY STARS
Find out who they really are!

WHO'S NEARLY FORTY—BUT STILL NAUGHTY?
The answer's inside!

AUSTRALIA 57c NEW ZEALAND 55c
MALAYSIA $1.50 IR 34p (inc. VAT)

The Best of

VOLUME 1

Frank Hopkinson

ROBSON
BOOKS

First published in the United Kingdom in 2006 by
Robson Books
151 Freston Road
London
W10 6TH

An imprint of Anova Books Company Ltd.

Copyright *My Guy* magazine/Frank Hopkinson, 2006.
My Guy magazine is a trademark of Perfectly Formed Publishing.

The moral right of the author has been asserted.

All rights reserved. No part of this publication may be reproduced, stored in a retrieval system, or transmitted in any form or by any means electronic, mechanical, photocopying, recording or otherwise, without the prior written permission of the copyright owner.

The feature spreads from this book were originally published in 1978. No alteration has been made to their content and so the addresses for both editorial and advertising features are no longer relevant. No correspondence should be sent to the original publishers, IPC Magazines. Further information may be obtained from www.myguymag.co.uk.

Acknowledgements: Thanks to the early staff of *My Guy*; Gaythorne Silvester, Bridget Callaghan (Julie), John Harding (Bob), Mary Hatchard (Andy), Kaye Goddard, Sue Teddern, Norah McGrath, June Welch, Eve Lynn-Hill, Hamish Dawson, Sophie Tilley, Susan Welby, Christine Bivand, Suzy Smith, Karen Foster, Gary Rice, Maureen Rice, Debbie Voller, Fiona Soutar, Simon Geller and David Day.
Plus photo-story photographers: Gary Compton, Karin Simons, Mike Prior, David Watts, Henry Arden and Sven Arnstein.

ISBN 1 86105 979 5

A CIP catalogue record for this book is available from the British Library.

10 9 8 7 6 5 4 3 2 1

Printed in China

Contents

If social historians want to trace the roots of lad-ette culture back to some starting point, then March 1978 might be a good place. *My Guy* arrived at the newsagents, a new weekly magazine for teenage girls who liked boys, clothes, photo-stories and…um boys. *My Guy* was fun and funky and for girls on the pull. *Jackie* at the time was regarded as 'slightly safe' and would include sensible features about careers to appease anxious parents. *My Guy* was unashamedly trivial, and a boyfriend was a must-have accessory.

The magazine was supposedly put together by Julie (the Ed), Bob (the Deputy Ed) and Andy (the Pop Reporter). In real life Julie was journalist Deirdre Vine who would go on to edit *Woman's Journal*, while Bob was actually called Bob and worked as a paste-up artist in the Youth Group.

After its launch *My Guy* was selling 300,000 copies a week and the new sensation, photo-stories, instantly drove *Jackie* to convert its drawn strip, full of gypsies with earrings luring girls at the fair, to run a photo-story of their own.

IPC magazines, the company behind *My Guy*, took no time at all to realise the potential of photo-stories and converted *Pink*, *Mates*, *Oh Boy* and even *Fab 208* into photo-story titles, while launching *Photo Love* and the even racier *Photo Secret Love*. But *My Guy* was king and outsold and outlasted them all, even *Jackie*. The novelty of photo-stories wore off in the mid-80s as teenagers got more sophisticated. Television started to produce soaps featuring teenagers, there was *Home & Away* and *Neighbours* to catch up with every day, and fiction virtually disappeared from magazines. IPC sold off *My Guy* in 1995 and it struggled on as a monthly until it finally folded in 2000 after 22 years.

Frank Hopkinson

CELEBRITY PHOTO-STORIES – WE'VE GOT 'EM!

The Best of My Guy Volume I brings you the features and adverts of 1978 along with photo-stories from the first five years. There should be some familiar faces to spot; Tracey Ullman appeared in many stories before getting her big TV break, Hugh Grant turned up in the same holed jumper and overcoat for most of his photo-story career, while George Michael was due to star with Wham! partner Andrew Ridgeley but Andrew couldn't get out of bed, and so George's mate David Austin stepped in at the last minute. Tony Hadley used to work over the road from IPC in the business press division and was nabbed by the magazine staff. Actresses Alex Kingston, Saskia Reeves, Francesca (*'Allo 'Allo*) Gonshaw, Caroline Gruber, Cindy Shelley and Sarah-Jane Varley were all PhotoPix models recruited through drama school noticeboards. Cindy and Sarah-Jane both ended up in *Howard's Way* along with photo-story 'hunk' Edward Highmore, who played Leo. You might also notice *Coronation Street*'s Sally Webster (actress Sally Whittaker), Elizabeth Garvie (Eliza Bennett in BBC's 1980 *Pride & Prejudice*) starring with Peter Chelsom who went on to direct *Hear My Song*, and Tim Marriott from *The Brittas Empire*.

Sadly there was no space to feature former royal dress designer and now successful novelist, Bella Pollen, though given her choice of career, she probably regrets the clothes.

OUT OF THE DARKNESS

I started working on the magazine as a photo-story writer in 1980, having received the perfect training for it – a degree in environmental studies from the agricultural college of London University. My very first story was a four-part serial *Out of the Darkness*, starring a nineteen-year-old Alex Kingston, later to find fame as Moll Flanders and Dr Elizabeth Corday in *ER*. The photographer on this particular job was the inexhaustibly enthusiastic Gary Compton. Gary's driving was always a concern to those in the front passenger seat, because he would split his attention equally between the person he was talking to and what was happening on the road in front. The passengers would communicate vehicles stopping in front of him by staring ahead and widening their eyes.

The models for this story arrived in Wye, Kent, after a 100mph journey down the M20 with Gary enthusing wildly about Alex's pre-Raphaelite hair and all of them in a state of mild shock. Photo-story model agent Hemma Sullivan had cast it perfectly. Hemma ran an agency called PhotoPix from her home in Kingston. She combined jolly hockeysticks charm with utter frankness, 'Darling, tell me, are you terribly spotty at the moment?'

Alex was the innocent and vulnerable girl left alone in an isolated cottage; there was the good looking boyfriend, the raffish cad who would try and seduce her, and the out-and-out nutter who was just itching to turn the power off and get strangling.

We spent all day shooting the scenes in and around student houses that were loaned to the agricultural college I'd just left – one for the exterior and one for the interior. Gary took particular care to get the available light shots right in the darkness sequences and some of the frames were shot at half a second. Then, after a long day his Braun flash pack expired and we had to shoot the last three or four frames with direct flash (most of the lighting effects you see in photo-stories are from light bounced onto walls and ceilings).

Alex was very quiet throughout the story, but the strip of photos from the contact sheet – none of which we actually used in the magazine – gives you an indication of how she could switch on 'hysterical' in seconds.

Having imagined I would be working on *My Guy* for at most a couple of years, I ended up as editor and then buying the magazine from IPC in 1995. However, rest assured that teenage photo-stories haven't entirely disappeared – Belgian magazine, *Joepie* still runs a weekly photo-serial.

MY GUY

ISSUE 6   8 APRIL 1978

Seen our pull-out this week? It's worth a bomb! Now next time you see Rod Stewart you can flash your Blackmail Book at him and just open up your shopping bag for him to stuff with fivers. Eyes down now and a quick look in at . . .

MY GUY'S INSIDES!

Published every Saturday by IPC Magazines Ltd King's Reach Tower, Stamford Street, London, SE1 9LS. Sole agents: Australia and New Zealand, Gordon & Gotch; South Africa, Central News Agency Ltd: Rhodesia & Zambia, Kingston Ltd. All rights reserved and reproduction without permission strictly forbidden. Photographs posed by models. Printed in England. ©IPC Magazines Ltd. 1978.

TALKING TO

Bob'll soon need glasses, Julie's cracked a rib and Andy's rolling around on the floor! Is it the food here? No, they've been reading all your nutty letters, that's all! So please keep 'em rolling in and us rolling about at *My Guy*, 21st Floor, King's Reach Tower, Stamford Street, London, SE1 9LS. We pay £2 for each one printed and £5 for a real cracker!

KEEP FAT!
What's plump, red in the face, out of breath, worn out, starving hungry, exhausted and bloomin' miserable?

Answer, me! After me first and last Keep Fit class! It was more like an army assault course!

Cor! They can keep that! From now on I'm concentrating on keeping fat!

Dimply Bum, Portsmouth.

FRUITY!
I reckon I've got the worst Saturday job in the world. You see, I help out on a greengrocer's stall in a market.

Fellas swarm round like fruit flies — just to be rude!

If I hear one more comment like: "That's a nice pear you've got there luv" or "Lettuce have some fun together" someone really is going to end up with a cauliflower ear!

Janey, E. London.
Get many dates, do ya?

SILLY MOO!
"You know," whispered my ever-romantic fella, "your eyes are just like Daisy's."

"Daisy who?" I said leaping up.

"Oh, don't worry about her love," he replied. "She was a cow my dad won first prize with once."

Huh! I think I would have preferred it if he had been two-timing me!

Penny, Yorkshire.

EAT YOUR WORDS
I spotted this book the other day called "How To Lose Weight — Method Guaranteed."

As it was only 10 pence, I coughed up.

Guess what it said inside? STOP EATING! I was so cross I nearly ate the book!

Maria, Eastbourne.

DOGGONE!
What do you call a greyhound who sells ice cream? Easy. Mr. Whippit of course!

I made that one up myself!

Chrissy, Bath.
Really? We'd never have

MY GUY'S RECORDS!

This week, Kevin Matthews, who's got a head-start as record-holder for: THE WORLD'S MOST REVOLTING HAIR TO RUN YOUR HANDS THROUGH!

Jane Rowlands of Hackney, his courageous (mad?) girlfriend, writes:

"Kev thinks he'll get brain damage if he washes his hair. His barnet practically walks round on its own! Run yer fingers through that matted mop and you could lose yer hand and be smothered by a halo of fleas . . .

I decided I'd have to give him up today — I've just noticed even his dandruff's black!"

Send in the record you think your guy holds and he will be immortalised. Even better, you'll be £2 richer if we print it!

guessed. Do us a favour Chrissy, if we send you two quid no more jokes! Please!

IN THE DARK
Last time I ever bother being considerate. I came in really late the other night and so as not to wake the others I didn't put any lights on.

All went well till I went to brush my fangs.

Uugh! I'd squeezed a tube of hair remover by mistake. Now I've got a tongue like Kojak!

Sara, Burnley.

A WEE BOOB!
My daft mate came out from a marathon session in a public loo grinning from lug 'ole to lug 'ole.

"Cor!" she said. "Those loos aren't half good. They even provide umbrella stands."

Found out the daft bat had gone into the gents by mistake. Now I know why she took so long!

Jackie, Lee Green.

DAILY FUN
My fella does a newspaper round and delivers my dad's papers. So as a joke (!) one morning I left a note on the door saying: "C'mon up darlin' and give us a kiss!" Fell a bit flat though. 'Cos Brian had gone ill that day and his boss found my note. He gives me a funny look whenever he sees me now.

(No wonder — he's over 60)!

Maureen, Manchester.

CHEST A MINUTE!
I had suspected bronchitis, so there I was, stripped to the waist in our doctor's surgery.

"Humph," he coughed, as he prodded me with his stethoscope. "You are a bit chesty aren't you?"

Did he really want an answer?!

Gayle, Avon.
We thought Andy was the only fella who made 'boobs' like that!

TOUPEE OR NOT TOUPEE?
Feeling a bit bored the other day, I was going through our family photo albums.

I found lots of pics of this tall skinny bloke. He was real yukky. Four eyes and bald as a coot!

Wetting meself laughing, I showed 'em to mum and asked who the other fella in her life was.

Just as well dad was at work, for my sake.

Turned out it was him in his pre-contact lens and toupee days!!

Marie, Fife.

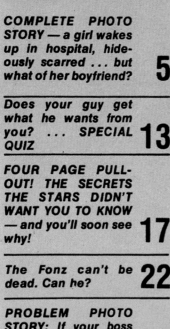

MY GUY

THE £5 BETTER LETTER

BIG MOUTH!

I got a really strange present from my fella the other day — gob stoppers!

"What d'ya buy these for?" I asked.

"To shut you up for one minute," was the icy reply. "I've been trying to tell you we're finished for the last hour, but you wouldn't let me get a word in."

Some loss. I mean, everyone knows I prefer bubble gum!

Lucy, Telford.

WANNA DO YOUR FACE A FAVOUR?? TURN TO P.10 AND GRAB HOLD OF OUR GIVEAWAY!

MOUSTAKE!

My mum's a bingo freak and gets herself in a real state over it. Especially if she thinks she's winning.

She really raised the roof the other day though. Her last number was called and in the excitement she called out mousey instead of housey!

Then, the silly woman next to her jumped on to her chair screaming!

Best thing was though, Mum had heard the number wrong anyway!

Gillian, Chatham.
Ratted on 'em all didn't she!

HAPPINESS IS PINT SHAPED!

My boyfriend was — how can I put this — rather fond of his pint. And he was always coming round to see me after he'd had one too many.

To cure him — I thought I'd have a sip of me mum's cooking sherry to see how he liked me reeking of booze for a change! Trouble was it went straight to my head and I just sat and giggled all night.

That was the last time I saw him. I got a note the next day saying: 'Sorry — I can't stand girls who drink'!!

Katie, Blackheath.
Quite right. I can't stand 'em either . . . I usually let 'em fall over!!! — Bob.

TWO BOB A JOB!

My mate and I belong to this youth club and just lately they've gone all social conscious. You know, tidying old people's gardens and that.

We got roped into getting the shopping for one little old lady. So one Saturday morning, feeling ever so good, we set off for her list.

Was she grateful?

No — told us her sister always got her shopping and offered us 10 pence to go away!

Caroline, Maidstone.

SUPER MUM

My mum is dead superstitious. We're not allowed to put our shoes on the table and she won't let us pick up our gloves if we drop them!

But the best thing of all is that, at the moment, Mum — *not us* — is sitting in bed nursing a broken ankle . . .

Well, that's not very funny I know. But she broke it tripping over our cat!

His name's Blackie y'see and guess what colour he is???!

June, Whitburn.

TAKE YOUR PIC!

Send us your funny photos and potty Polaroids — £5 for every one printed!

ALL THE FUN (?) OF THE FAIR

How do you like this Chamber of Horrors then? It's my friends Mary, Maxien and I on our way back from the fair. Only trouble is, everyone keeps telling me it's the best piccie I've ever had taken!

Lousie, Co. Durham.
We'd hate to see ya worst!

You want 'em — we've got 'em. Yep! Some of the tastiest fellas in the country — and just waiting to hear from you! And you guys, remember we pay £2 for every picture published!

Hi Guys!

Think you could get on target with David Wenham? His fave hobby is shooting and flying. He's 17, 5' 10½" and his ideal girl is tall and curvy with very long hair. If you're definitely NOT into punk, he wants to hear from you

Britain's answer to Nick Nolte could be yours! All the way from Surrey we bring to you 17 year old James Fairburn who loves skin-diving. He likes camping, so if you're the outdoor sort, get writing

If you fancy a fast mover James Wiches, 17, is the guy for you. He's just crazy about motorbikes and slim, elegant(!) young ladies. So if you're around 16 and 5' 5", drop a line

Here's a fella with his head firmly in the clouds. Trev Woods' hobby is plane spotting. If you reckon you could bring this 5' 10" blue eyed, blond hunk down to earth, write to him

Howdya fancy getting your hooks into John Talyor? He's a keen fisherman but his favourite catch would be 5' 4", tasty and slim. So if you wanna get in before the other worms write quick!

Here's a fella who looks after his body. He's into keep fit, travelling and sport. But he's gonna spend some of his time on you! Gary Buckley's the name and he's 5' 6" with dark hair and eyes.

♥ S.W.A.L.K. ♥

Do you wanna let someone know how you feel — or how you wanna feel? Send your message to us (at the address above) and we'll guarantee they get to know about it!

EVER SO HOT!

HOT LIPS — Keep all those kisses for me — I'll be back to get 'em real soon. — Kev, Belfast.
JAMIE — Everyone's still talking about what we did — great isn't it? Naughty Nell
DAVE B. LANCS — And to think I used to go to the cinema for the choc ices. Back row Betty.
BOY IN SOUTHAMPTON TOP RANK — Please wave next time. Sorry I giggled. 'Red Dress.'

EVER SO TENDER!

S. D. FOLKESTONE — Missin' you, lovin' you, wantin' you more each day. Roll on Summer. Steve.
HAIRY HANDS, DORSET — When I fall in love it'll be forever. So it looks like you're stuck with me. Emma.
J. D. — The only good thing about this world at the moment is you. Stay with me and kiss it better. John.

EVER SO CUDDLY!

RED RIDING HOOD — There's no need to be afraid — little girls give me indigestion — Big Bad Wolf.
LEGGY LINDA — Who loves ya baby? I do — always. Kojak
PETER WILSON NORTH YORKS — Anybody out there going out with him? If so, leave off. He's mine. Gerry Franks.

Sealed With A Loving Kiss X

TV Fun TIMES

We've got 'em all — the gorgeous, the gruesome and anything that's good for a giggle on TV!

Another TV cracker to turn on to!

BECK (INSALE) AND CALL!

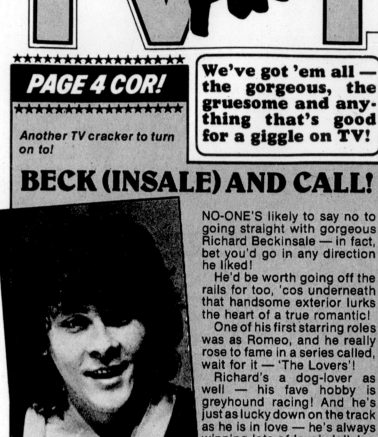

NO-ONE'S likely to say no to going straight with gorgeous Richard Beckinsale — in fact, bet you'd go in any direction he liked!

He'd be worth going off the rails for too, 'cos underneath that handsome exterior lurks the heart of a true romantic!

One of his first starring roles was as Romeo, and he really rose to fame in a series called, wait for it — 'The Lovers'!

Richard's a dog-lover as well — his fave hobby is greyhound racing! And he's just as lucky down on the track as he is in love — he's always winning lots of lovely lolly!

You just couldn't lose with him around!

TELLY TEASERS

If you can get this little lot right – you must have square eyes! So put yourself off the box by spending a special evening with Moira Anderson and Stars on Sunday!

1. Who sounds like a sneeze and is on sale with Old Nick Parsons?
2. There's two brassy, bitchy blondes behind the bar in Coronation Street. Name 'em!
3. And talking of pubs, what's the boozer in Emmerdale Farm called?
4. Think of a bionic classical composer!
5. Richard O'Sullivan's fallen on his feet with Tessa Wyatt, but what's his surname in Robin's Nest?
6. If you wanted to cross the Channel by tightrope, who'd fix it for you?
7. Where'd you find an Amateur Latin American? *(In a homemade poncho? — Andy).*
8. What has 12 legs, very little brain and makes most fellas weak at the knees?

TV TURN ONS...TV TURN OFFS...

'Why can't Esther Rantzen keep her trap shut? Every time our goldfish sees those gleaming gnashers, he goes green and hides behind his waterweed!' Belinda Hatchard, Sussex.

'... How does Cannon keep his figure?' Beanpole, Kent.

'I always thought Eddie Waring commentating was foreign interference...' Fiona, Cheshunt.

This week starring: Pam (it rhymes with ham) Ayres!

The place where we say, tough luck, to the folks who have to live with the stars *all* the time!

A BREATH OF FRESH AYRE SPRAY!

We'd like to say we're sorry,
To them country folks who dwell
With that grinning rural yokel
Called Pam Ayres, so we've heard tell.

She must be a terror to live with
'Cos of all them bloomin' rhymes,
Besides her bloomin' cheeks an' nose
What needs blowin' all the time!

She's ever so fond o' the country
With it's farmyard muck an' all.
"Oi uses that, and silage,
To stick me poems to the wall."

She goes everywhere in wellies,
That black rubber fair gits her goin' —
Down to the bottom o' the garden
To see how them parsnips is growin'!

Her 'air's her crownin' glory,
Hens use that as a nest,
"Oi don't need them posh conditioners,
'Cos farm-fresh eggs is best!"

★★★★★★★★★★★★★★★★★★★★★★★★
BACK IN A MINUTE!
The spot where we take a break for an ad!
HUNT THE LADY!

"Is it the way I walk? Or my long blond hair? Or 'cos I've been splashing Henry Cooper's scent on all over?

"Why *do* those two fellas keep calling me Jane?"

Yup! Poor ol' James Hunt definitely looks worried about his image in the Texaco ad, doesn't he?

Or maybe just about his engine?

Well, Jane — oops sorry, James — we can tell you you do look like a girlie, no, er, man!

After all the big one has got glasses and the short fat hairy one's got his wig in his eyes!

★★★★★★★★★★★★★★★★★★★★★★★★

TELLY TEASERS ANSWERS

Well, reckon you're in for a jolly time with Moira and her ton-sils! Why not cheat – it'd be much more enjoyable!

1. A-tish-oo! Sneh Gupta (What's in a name! She can hold my hanky any day! — Bob).
2. Gave you all the clues you needed! Bet Lynch & Annie Walker.
3. The Woolpack, complete with brassy blonde barmaid — Dolly Acaster!
4. Wagner! (Who?! — Andy).
5. Tripe, sorry, Tripp.
6. Doing the samba on 'Come Dancing'.
7. You guessed it (but Andy's still working on it) — Legs & Co.!

COMING SOON... *Silent movies are back — 'Whispering' Bob Harris gets laryngitis!*

MY GUY PHOTO STORY

OUT OF THE DARKNESS

Alone in the country. Carol had no reason to fear, but fear came out of the darkness

FINISHED, THE LAST ROOM FINISHED.

YES, I'VE JUST ABOUT HAD IT WITH POLYFILLA AND NON–DRIP EMULSIONS.

SO THAT'S YOUR EXCUSE FOR LEAVING ME ON MY OWN FOR A WHOLE WEEK.

NONSENSE — I HAVEN'T MOVED IN YET. I'M SAVING THAT FOR A MONTH'S TIME.

AND WHEN WE'RE MARRIED?

HOWLING WOLVES COULDN'T KEEP ME FROM THE DOOR.

DO YOU KNOW, WHEN THE WINDOWS RATTLE AT NIGHT, IT SOUNDS AS THOUGH SOMEONE'S TRYING TO GET IN.

IT'S JUST THE WIND, THE VALLEY FUNNELS IT DOWN HERE.

But Carol wasn't too sure.

YES, I KNOW, BUT IT STILL SOUNDS EERIE.

IT'S JUST YOUR IMAGINATION.

And no matter what she said, Graham was unconvinced.

Turn to page 41

BOOTS OFF, NO

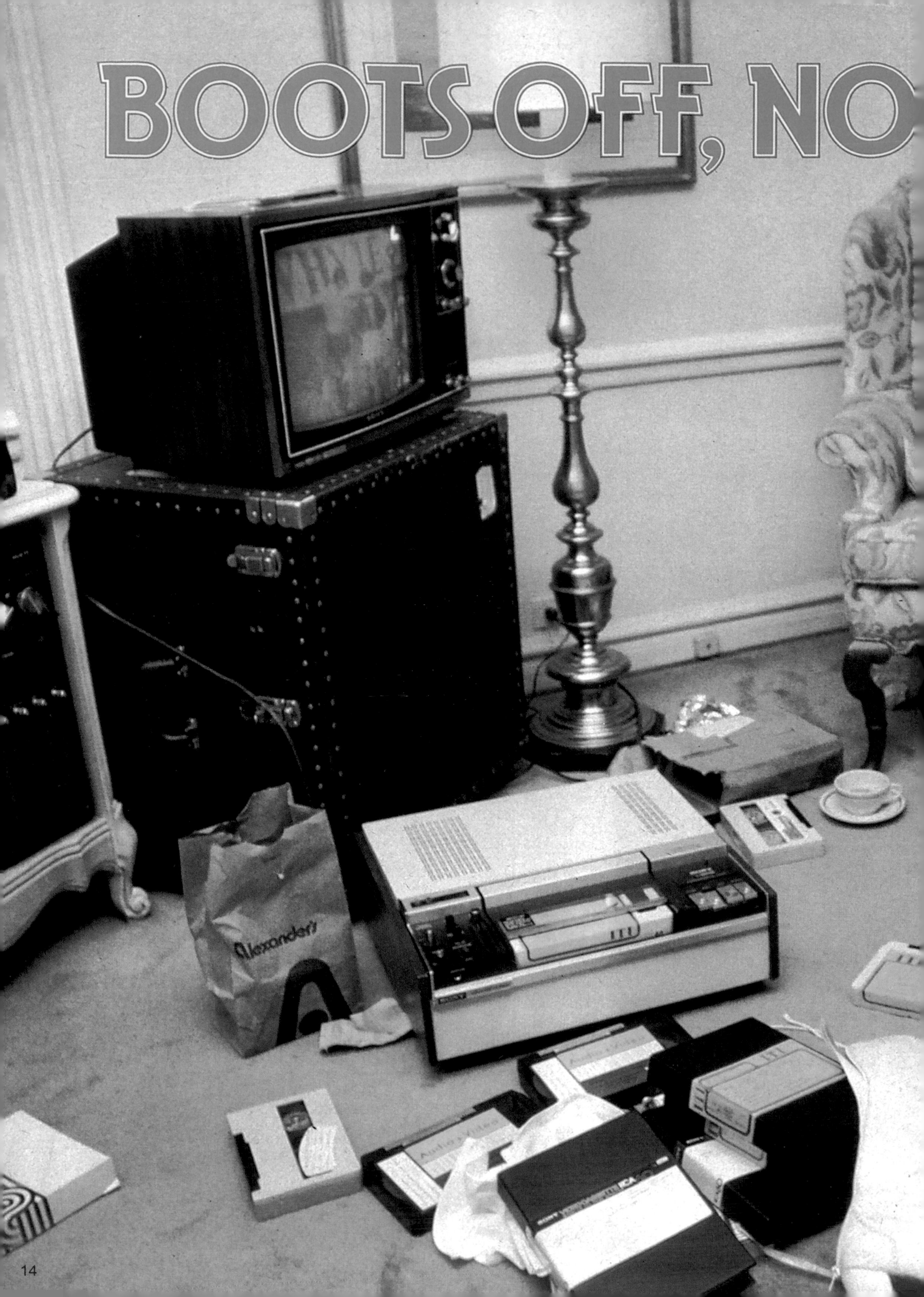

BIRDS...IT'S BLISS!

Rod's a stay-at-home lad, really. Stick him in front of a video film of Scotland thrashing England, gently pull his white leather boots off and then he'll tuck those great hairy legs under him and forget you exist!

Must've been tough for Britt and Co. hanging round in their frillies waiting for the lad to budge from that set... especially when he insists on using his own action replay — to watch the whole match over again!

Still, if you can't enjoy yourself when you're a superstar, what's the world coming to, eh Rod?

Rod? Rod! Oh, forget it...!

NO LAW'S GOING TO STOP ME WEARING WHAT I WANT TO WEAR.

SHORTS BY ACE, T-SHIRT AND SOCKS SLICK WILLIE'S, FREEDOM BY PANTY PADS.
YOU JUST PRESS THEM INTO YOUR PANTIES AND AN ADHESIVE STRIP KEEPS THEM SNUG AND NEAT.
SO NOTHING'S GOING TO STOP YOU WEARING WHAT YOU WANT TO WEAR.
FOR FREE SAMPLE WRITE TO LILIA-WHITE (PMG1), B'HAM B8 3DZ, STATING REGULAR SUPER, OR NEW SUPER PLUS.

MY GUY COMPLETE LOVE STORY

TOMORROW IS THE FIRST DAY...

Louise was just a lonely face at the window to Gareth... but inside her was a heart that had withered and died.

I'M LATE FOR WORK. I COULD STILL MAKE IT IF I TOOK THE SHORT CUT...

But I knew I wasn't going to do it

There was a street I had to go down...

NUMBER FIFTY TWO...FOURTH WINDOW ON THE LEFT...

A face I had to see...

THERE SHE IS!

It was over in seconds...

IT'S CRAZY...BUT I COULDN'T BEAR NOT TO SEE HER EVERY MORNING NOW. SHE'S BECOME PART OF MY LIFE...

Confessions of A... CLEVER KNICKS!

Okay, all you undie cover agents — we've got you taped! And we've got you some pretty natty knicks, too! Pick the ones you fancy and we'll tell you what they say about you — and where to get them, natch!

Oooh, la, la! You're a scorcher! Black French knicks (£1.80) by Sunarama from large dept. stores. Sexy shoes to match, Dolcis, £8.99.

Teaser! You love to lead 'em on! 'Satisfaction Guaranteed' knicks by Quant (70p) from large dept. stores. Vesty top by Wolsey (£2.90), sizes medium, large from Bourne & Hollingsworth, Bonds of Norwich and all Chiesman branches.

Starlet! You're cute . . . and cuddlesome! Silky knicks by Quant (60p), most big stores. Matching pink t-shirt from branches of Top Shop (£2.99). See-through shoes, Dolcis, £11.99.

Purr-fect! Tarzan'd love ya! Leopard print knicks by Quant (65p). One shoulder top by Plaza (£3.00) from Plaza, 341 Kings Rd., London SW3 (50p extra mail order).

Striper! You're a warm an' wonderful person! 'Specially in these stripey towelling knicks by Quant (75p). Top by Wolsey (who'd have guessed it's a vest?!), £2.00, stockists as above.

All prices approximate.

FUZZ OFF!

All right, hands, arms, legs up — who's got hairy ones! We all have! There's no getting away from the fuzz — and no point slipping into those sexy knicks and slinky tops if your underarms and legs aren't silky smooth to match! So, get it off!!

Quickest, neatest way to get legs smooth and hair-free is to shave 'em! You need a steady hand and your own razor — not Dad's! Get a good, soapy lather up and get to work *carefully*. Lots of good razors in your local chemists. Or, if you're in the money, try the battery operated Boots Lady Shaver (£7.95).

Faces get fuzz too! Usually just above the top lip, but *don't* use a razor here, please! Bleach it instead and it won't show at all. You can buy a very good creme bleach called Jolan at most chemists for £1.70 — sounds a lot but it lasts ages! Follow the instructions *carefully* and your face will look fine!

Underarms can be shaved but you might find it leaves a shadow — not nice! So, instead, try a cream hair remover — easy to use and much gentler. Boots do their own which comes in a tube (39p) and a lotion (45p). Again, follow instructions *carefully* and don't use if you have a rash or it stings a lot. Can be used on your legs, too!

SISTER BLACKMAIL!

It only takes a camera and an evil mind to turn one innocent kiss into a jealous sister's weapon of hate!

My fella, Gary, was really down — and he had a good reason . . .

. . .AND THE DOCTOR SAID THAT MUM'S GOT A WEAK HEART. ANY KIND OF SHOCK MIGHT. . . BE TOO MUCH FOR HER

OH, GARY, I — I'M SORRY. . .

THANKS, JUNE. IT'S NOT REALLY SUCH A SHOCK, THOUGH. SHE'S NEVER BEEN WELL SINCE DAD DIED LAST YEAR . . .

BUT IF SHE TAKES THINGS EASY, SHE'LL BE FINE, WON'T SHE ?

YEAH — I SUPPOSE I'M JUST WORRYING FOR NOTHING . . .

But when we stood up to go . . .

THAT'S ALL WE NEED! NOW IT'S STARTING TO RAIN !

I HOPE SO, GARY — IT'S AWFUL TO SEE YOU SO SAD

MY HOUSE IS NEAREST — WE'D BETTER RUN. LOOKS LIKE IT'S GOING TO BE HEAVY. . .

COME ON, I'M GETTING SOAKED !

WELL, I'M NOT WATER-PROOF, YOU KNOW. . .

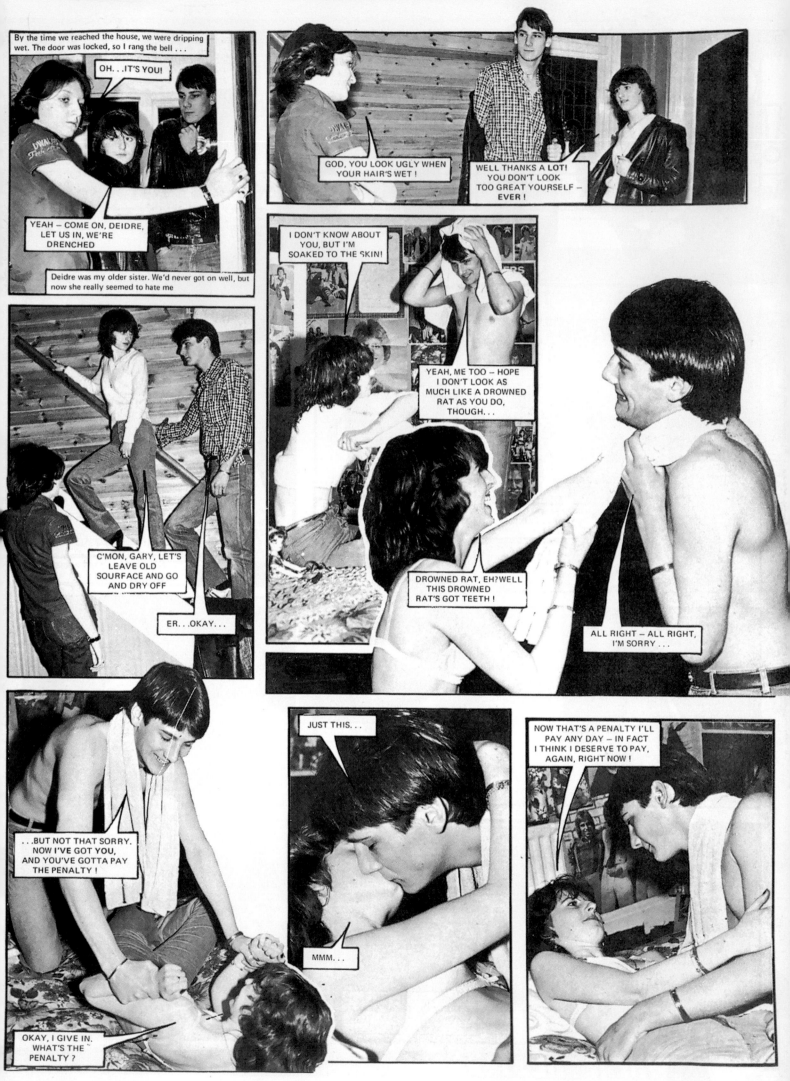

24

FULL COLOUR POSTERS

ABBA 35p
ALI 45p
SCREENSCENE
LINDSAY WAGNER 45p
KATE JACKSON 35p
FARRAH .1. 35p
JACLYN SMITH 45p
D. SOUL .1. 35p
STARSKY & HUTCH 35p
P. GLASER 25p
FONZ .2. 35p
FONZ .1. 35p
SEX PISTOLS 45p
IN MEMORY £1.00
SUPERSTAR ELVIS 45p
LINDSAY £1.00
OSMONDS £1.00
FONZ ON CYCLE £1.00
ANGIE £1.00
SUPER FARRAH £2.00
JACLYN £1.00
SUPER JACKSON £2.00
K. KEEGAN 25p
LIVERPOOL 25p
MAN. UTD. 25p
ELTON JOHN (s) £2.00
BRUCE LEE (s) £2.00
FONZ (s) £2.00

Allow 14 days for delivery.

25p 23" x 16"   35/45p 32" x 23"
£1.00 28" x 20"   £2.00 28" x 20"
(S) Super Felt Finish

Name ....

Address ....
....
....

Add 15p per poster for P&P (3 or more posters — P&P Free). Send now to:-

EVERYTHING YOU

Yep, we asked 'em! And (surprise, surprise!) they answered! Now we've got everything you need to know about 6 guys we'd all love to get close to!

WHAT D'YOU THINK OF..?

LES

DAVID

	LES	DAVID
Girls who pose in the nude?	Love 'em! Only trouble is I get so behind in the news. I never get past Page Three of the paper!	I wouldn't like my girl to do it — unless it was just for me!
Kissing — do you like it or prefer something else?	Kissing's great, so long as you don't get a slobberer! Personally I prefer 10p's worth of wet cod to a dribbler!	Guess I'll keep on doing it till they invent something better!
Big bosoms (on girls!)?	Well, I'm not against them (tho' I wouldn't mind!). I like a girl with a bit of padding (natural!) — yes, siree!	Never mind the width — feel the quality! I mean, it's not size that matters, it's having a nice shape, right?
Current fashions?	Bring back the mini skirt and standing under bus stairs!	I love the way girls all wear jeans these days. There's nothing nicer than a good bum in real tight jeans!
Sex symbols — would you like to meet one and (gulp!) why?	I'd like to meet Britt. I'd show her what a real Scotsman's made of!	I like them from afar — but I wouldn't like to meet one, say like Brigitte Bardot. She'd never match my fantasy!
Girls who come on strong, chat you up, ask you out?	Well, it saves you the trouble — so long as she's nice looking. Ugly ones? Well, I usually run!	I prefer 'em a bit more subtle. Y'know, they don't actually say anything — but you can tell right away they fancy you!
Going steady. D'you stick to one girl or go in for two-timing?	Nothing beats going steady with one girl — 'cept maybe going steady with two!	It's the nicest thing there is — so long as it doesn't get too steady!
Brainy girls — ones who aren't dumb, can talk and have minds?	Not too brainy. I mean you gotta be able to fool 'em in to doing what you want!	I hate dumb girls! Every time you meet a pretty girl she's got a bird-brain!
Love. Do you love it?	I love being in love. Just so long as it doesn't last too long . . .	There should be more of it! Specially for me!
Marriage. Do you fancy it?	No thanks. Not yet! Maybe when I'm older — if I meet the right girl.	I've tried it, and I guess some day I will again. But you have to know your partner very well first.
First dates — are they fun?	I hate 'em. I wish you could always start on the second one! It's O.K. if the chat flows easily, then it's dead exciting.	I get butterflies in my stomach and my heart pounds. It's great! When else do you feel like that about a girl?
Going out with 'the boys' — instead of a girl!	I love it. I mean girls are great — but they just don't play darts as well, do they?	It can be fun. I don't like drunken stag nights. Give me a girl on her own any day!

EVER WANTED TO ASK...

IAN   LEIF   PAUL   & MIDGE

IAN	LEIF	PAUL	& MIDGE
I just wish I was a photographer. They always say no when I show them my little instamatic!	I like 'em. I mean they have to be good lookers to get asked, don't they? If a girl of mine did it, I'd be proud!	*I don't like it too much; not when they show everything. I wouldn't like my girl to do it.*	Love looking at 'em, but I wouldn't want to marry one!
I prefer having my back massaged. If somebody'd do that and kiss me as well . . . know any double-jointed girls?	Nothing better! Can't beat a tender, loving kiss . . .	**Love it! Saves talking to her, doesn't it?!**	There's no better way to start a relationship!
Not fussy. A girl's a girl, after all!	Not really big ones — they frighten me! Specially if they're jumping out of a dress like they're gonna attack you!	*I hate 'em! I prefer little ones. Big ones make me feel like I'm being dominated!*	They're nice — so long as they aren't, y'know, droopy!
I like minis — the sort that come down to a girl's chin. But not when she's got legs like a tree trunk!	Everybody wears jeans and girls dress like fellas. I like a girl to wear something more feminine . . . like a dress!	*I love tight leather trousers. I hated mini skirts, 'cos very few girls have got good enough legs to wear them!*	I like current fashions 'cos of all the bright colours people are wearing, they're great!
I do rather like Farrah. Just wonder how I'd get Lee out of the way tho' . . .	I'd like to meet Sophia Loren, just to see if those great big eyes are for real.	*Brigitte Bardot. I'd be so knocked out just meeting her that I'd be lost for words. Mind you, I wouldn't want to talk!*	There aren't many sex symbols left. I wouldn't have minded meeting Marilyn Monroe at her best!
Do girls really do that? Show me some, just show me some!	I run away from 'em!	*I hate it. When I meet a girl like that I usually suddenly remember that I'm s'posed to be somewhere else and leave!*	I love 'em. It saves you the trouble. I'm hopeless at chatting girls up.
I am a firm believer in only going out with one girl at a time. One for Saturday, one for Sunday . . .	It's nice. Besides, I can't handle more than one girl at a time. S'pose I *could* try . . .	*I did go steady a long time ago, but my work makes it impossible — you're never in one place long enough!*	It's okay if you like that kinda thing. Personally I prefer playing around a bit!
You have to have 'O' levels to go out with me — in snogging of course!	It's no use a girl just looking good. She's gotta be able to talk too. It gets boring just looking at a girl!	*I like them. Not too brainy, mind you. I like to know what they're talking about!*	**Uh-oh. Not too brainy! Medium to dumb, I like 'em!**
When it happens to me, I'll believe in it. Till then . . . I'll have fun!	I've been in love lots of times. In fact I'm always in love with somebody or something!	*I've never been in love. I s'pose I might be one day, but not at the moment 'cos I'm having too much fun!*	It hasn't happened to me yet. I'll wait till it does — you know, rockets going off, bells ringing, that kinda thing!
Probably one day. I'd like to settle down sometime.	**Hmm, not just yet, thanks. Ask me again in another ten years!**	*I believe in it, so I suppose it'll happen one day when I meet 'Miss Right'!*	Not yet. Maybe when I'm 35, bald and driving a bus I'll get wed to anyone who'll have me!
The bad thing about first dates is you're always wondering if they're gonna be last one too!	They're terrible — you never know what to do, or where she wants to go, or if you're boring the pants off her!	*I don't get nervous, but I'm out to impress and appear super-cool. I'm not really myself, so I don't have that much fun.*	Well, I don't talk much, so if she doesn't talk much we end up counting the patterns on the wallpaper!
I love it. I have a great time. But sometimes I wonder why we always end up talking about girls!	It's cheaper than going out with a girl — fellas always pay their share!	*Yeah, I prefer going out with my mates — to pubs or Turkish baths. Or chatting up girls!*	There's times you've gotta have female company, and others when you just want a good laugh with your mates!

THE LOVING VASE

When Janie spotted a vase in a shop, she knew she had to have it – but she didn't know it would change her life...

I'd stopped to look in the window of an antique shop.

I LIKE THAT OLD VASE. IT WOULD LOOK REALLY NICE IN MY BEDROOM AT HOME.

Inside. . .

CAN I HELP YOU?

MMM. . .HE CERTAINLY ISN'T AN ANTIQUE!

I WAS WONDERING ABOUT THAT VASE IN THE WINDOW – BUT I SUPPOSE IT'S PRETTY EXPENSIVE?

DEPENDS ON WHO'S BUYING. I SOMETIMES LET THINGS GO CHEAP TO SPECIAL CUSTOMERS.

BESIDES, THIS ISN'T JUST AN ORDINARY VASE, Y'KNOW. THE OLD LADY I GOT IT FROM CALLED IT HER LOVING VASE.

WHAT DOES THAT MEAN?

THERE'S MORE LOVING IN MY GUY

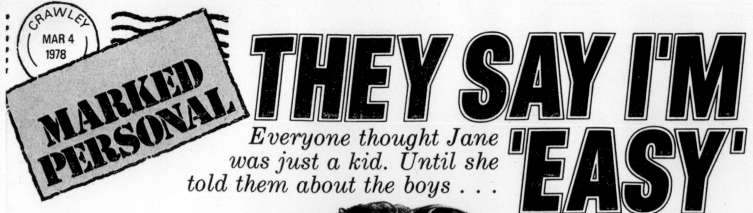

THEY SAY I'M 'EASY'

Everyone thought Jane was just a kid. Until she told them about the boys . . .

IT ALL started as a bit of a giggle, really.

Well, the crowd of girls who were my mates were always going on about what they'd done with their boyfriends, how this guy had kissed them, or that guy had tried to undo her skirt or something. And I used to get sick of hearing it all.

I didn't have a regular fella of my own. In fact, I hadn't really had very many dates, so when the conversation got round to boys, I always felt left out of it. One or two of the girls even made rotten little remarks about how Jane didn't know what they were talking about — so I started to dream up stories of the imaginary guys I'd been with.

"Of course Ron," I'd say, "had me in the back of his car. He was pulling at my clothes and if this policeman hadn't come along and knocked on the roof, I hate to think what might've happened! I tell you, I'm lucky to be here in one piece!"

TOUGH

They all looked at me, that first night, and there was something different in their faces. Suddenly I wasn't just 'poor old Jane' any more. I was somebody who'd got into what could've been a really tough situation — and come out of it alive!

I really enjoyed those looks. It made me feel as if I belonged in the group, as if I wasn't just an outsider any more.

So when I *did* have dates, I couldn't wait to meet the rest of the girls and embroider on what had *actually* happened. They all lapped it up, and the more detail they asked for — the more I gave them, until I practically believed half my stories myself.

I got quite a reputation for knowing how to handle fellas as well and when I started dating Ken regularly, I used to rush in to the girls next day and tell them everything that had gone on.

Of course, most of it was lies — Ken was a really nice guy — but my mates didn't know that.

I made it all sound really good — as if I'd been out with a load of guys and knew every trick in the book — and I knew the girls used to talk about it themselves when I wasn't there.

The funny thing was, they didn't talk about their *own* experiences so much any more. They seemed to be quite pleased just to listen to the next episode of what had happened to me.

Of course, I never even *hinted* to Ken that I was spreading these stories around. When I was with him I was happy just to feel his arms round me; or to let him kiss

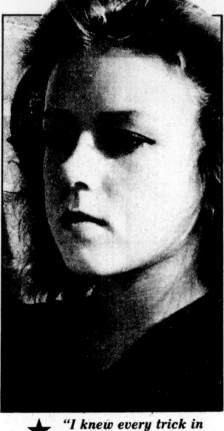

★ *"I knew every trick in the book . . ."*

me, but the once he tried to go a bit farther than that — I nearly slapped his face.

"I'm not that kind of girl!" I told him, and he gave me a funny, sideways look.

"That's not the way I've heard it recently," he mumbled. But then he smiled, took my hand and said he must've been mistaken. That the guy he'd been talking to must've meant a different Jane.

RAPED!

I was worried for a bit, but by the end of the week — when we were going to a party where I knew all my mates would be — I'd forgotten all about it.

Ken was getting drinks at the other side of the room and the usual mob of girls was round about me asking what had happened to me recently, so I bent my head forward and whispered, "You saw the guy I came in with? Well, last night, down by the quarry, he suddenly threw me onto the grass, pulled my clothes off and practically raped me! I was terrified. He threatened to do it again if I said anything or didn't bring him here tonight, so don't say a word, will you?"

There was a sudden silence in the group

— and I looked up.

Ken was standing there, staring at me as if I'd just crept out from under a stone.

"Yes," he said firmly, grinning nastily at the other girls. "It's quite true. But I didn't have to force her. She enjoyed every second of it. Or hasn't she told you that bit yet?" Then he turned on his heel and walked away.

Most of the faces round about me had gone white, and the girls were sort of looking at me as if they didn't know what to do or say. Then one by one they started to drift off.

I heard them talking about me just before I ran away from the party.

CHEAP

At first I couldn't see why they were all so shocked at what he'd said. After all it wasn't *that* much worse than the stories I'd been filling them with for weeks. And whenever I'd come out with one of my sexy episodes they hadn't acted shocked, they'd just lapped them up and asked for more!

So why didn't they want to know me now? I'd have thought that Ken's tale was just the sort of thing they all wanted to hear . . . But all at once the horrible truth hit me. They'd never really believed *my* stories, they'd thought it was all a bit of a giggle. But because Ken had overheard what I was making up about him and had been so disgusted — they believed *him*. They actually thought I was a cheap little tart who let boys do what they want to her!

I was so ashamed I didn't know what to do.

My old mates don't talk to me any more. It's as if I'm something dirty. They just turn away as soon as they see me coming.

As for the guys — well, they all think I'm easy, so any dates I have these days turn into all-in wrestling matches.

I suppose, sooner or later people'll start to forget about my stories. But *I* never will. And I've learned my lesson. In future I'll keep my mouth firmly shut about any decent guy who takes me out.

Always provided one ever does again, of course.

NEXT WEEK: *The girl who liked to make boys cry . . .*

Personal
MY GUY.
Kings Reach Tower,
Stamford Street,
London SE1. 9LS.

WHY CAN'T YOU BE IN LOVE LIKE THIS?

Well, maybe you can. Want to find out? Then try our very tender test — and find out if you're ready for love!

Part I: You

1. Are you ever afraid of falling in love? *Yes/No*

2. Have you met a boy yet that you thought you might like to marry? *Yes/No*

3. Are you pleased with the way you look? *Yes/No*

4. Do you find it easy to share things? *Yes/No*

5. Would you rather kiss a real boy than a pin-up? *Yes/No*

6. Have you ever thought younger girls silly for thinking they're in love? *Yes/No*

7. When you ask someone's opinion of yourself, do you really want to know the truth? *Yes/No*

8. Would you rather not do something than risk doing it badly? *Yes/No*

Part II: Him

9. Do you think most boys rate looks first, personality second?

10. Would you say 'no' to a boy if you knew your mates didn't like him? *Yes/No*

11. Is it important that a boy

love you as much as you loved him, would you finish the relationship? *Yes/No*

14. Is love less important to boys than girls? *Yes/No*

15. Do the girls he's been out with before matter to you? *Yes/No*

16. Would you say it's natural for most boys to go as far as they can, if a girl will let them? *Yes/No*

Part III: Together

17. Do you think it's possible to be really in love with someone you don't trust? *Yes/No*

18. If your parents didn't like your fella, would it matter very much to you? *Yes/No*

19. Can two totally different people fall in love? *Yes/No*

20. If you only saw your fella once a month (or less) do you think it would last? *Yes/No*

21. He's been off with another girl — can you forgive him? *Yes/No*

22. Is being married really important if you're in love? *Yes/No*

23. Would you still see your old mates once you'd got your guy? *Yes/No*

24. Do you ever think what you might do if you fell out of love with him? *Yes/No*

25. If you discovered something unpleasant about his past, would you be able to forget it? *Yes/No*

pays for you when you go out together? *Yes/No*

12. When a boy says he loves

her, should a girl believe him? *Yes/No*

13. If you thought he didn't

WELL, CAN YOU?

PART I:

If you answered **mostly 'Yes'** in this section you're ready and waiting to fall in love! You're very mature, sensible and prepared for the bad, as well as the good things that'll come your way — you reckon having a good relationship with a guy can be hard work as well as fun — and you're right! You're happy with yourself too, don't worry too much about not being perfect, just accept that you're YOU and any guy who comes along will have to learn to live with it. Great — all you need now is the guy!

If your answers were **mostly 'No'**, it seems likely you've already met the guy of your dreams . . . and he's stuck up on your bedroom

wall right now! You might not have thought seriously about one guy, but you dream a lot and reckon you'll know him when you see him! You worry a lot about yourself and sometimes wonder if there'll ever be a boy who loves YOU — don't worry, it'll happen when you're ready!

PART II:

Mostly 'Yes': When you do fall in love what'll the lucky boy be like? Well, if you have your way he'll be the most perfect creature ever to walk this earth! Kind, sensitive, caring but, most of all, good looking! You just won't accept second best — if he's not the boy you've been dreaming about, you'd rather just carry on dreaming. If you do find him though, he'll be a

pretty special guy — the sort of fella who can dominate you without you really noticing and who'll never look twice at another girl . . . because no-one else could compare to you.

Mostly 'No': The boy you fall in love with could be anybody! Anybody that is, who cares about a girl's feelings, who treats you like a person first and a girl second, who loves you and doesn't care what anyone else thinks. He won't necessarily have to be good-looking, but he will have to be mature, steady and honest. What you're looking for is someone you can really rely on and 'one-night standers' and flirts won't get very far with you!

PART III:

Mostly 'Yes': How do you see your ideal relationship? Well, for you just being one half of a couple

would be a pretty nice feeling, the warmth and security appeal to you and having a guy of your own would make you very happy. You might not fall madly, wildly, passionately in love but what you will achieve will be a steady, lasting relationship that other people will envy.

Mostly 'No': You're a romantic and, for you, being with a boy would have no meaning unless he was the only boy in the world you wanted to be with! You have a feeling in your heart that one day this sort of perfect love will happen to you and you're prepared to sacrifice a lot for it. You're stubborn too, and it's our bet you'd wait for ever for your perfect partner to come. It's your choice. Take a chance on a guy you're *not quite* sure of or wait for that special boy and maybe — just maybe — fall in love like you've always dreamed.

ME AND MY GUY

We want to know about you and your guy, so drop a line quick to the usual address!

EVER WANTED TO HUG HIM TO DEATH?

HE LEFT ME FOR A BLONDE!

I'd only been going out with Steve for a couple of weeks but it was long enough for us both to realise it was going to last.

Anyway, we went to this party together and I got talking to my mates. You know what it's like. I was showing off a bit about Steve and telling them how well we got on together. The next minute I turned round to point him out and there he was standing with his arm round a really sexy blonde.

All my mates were wetting themselves laughing. I rushed over to him fuming, all ready to tell him to get lost. Luckily, he got his bit in first.

"Claire," he said, "meet my sister, Sue, she's just come back from college. I didn't think she'd make it in time."

It took a couple of seconds to sink in by which time I had him in the tightest bear hug ever. I was almost in tears I was so happy. He's never found out what he did to deserve that one!

Claire, Manchester

TAKEN IN — BY THE TRUTH!

S'pose mine is the usual story really. I'd been out with a fella who'd done the dirty behind my back. In future, I thought, no one's gonna make a fool of me.

So, when Gary came on the scene I wasn't too surprised when, after a while, he said he couldn't see so much of me. First it was just Friday nights, then it stretched into whole weekends. He said he was

I COULD'VE KILLED HIM

Just before my last birthday Sammy had been leading me on something rotten about the lovely present he'd got me.

"It's going to alter our whole life together — it's really going to make a big difference," he told me with a big grin.

So imagine how I felt when I unwrapped a padded bra on my birthday. And in front of my Dad. The thank you hug he got very nearly did kill him!

He was right though — it did studying for exams. Well, I wasn't going to fall for that one again. So I used to go out with a whole crowd of mates and get off with any fella who asked me. I had a really great time.

When I did see Gary, I was friendly but a bit on the cool side. Anyway, one Friday night Gary arrived on the doorstep all dressed up. "C'mon love," he said. "Get ready, we're going out." Well, we arrived at this posh restaurant and he looked all dreamily into my eyes and said: "Thanks a lot Julie." "What for?" I asked. "For being so understanding about all the work I had to do.

"I heard today I've passed all my exams so we can get back to normal again."

Well, we didn't half get some odd looks from the other customers and waiters, but I

change our life — I chucked him the following day!

Angela, Scarborough

rushed round and sat on his lap and just hugged him for at least five minutes.

I'm so glad he never found out how little I really did understand!

Julie, Hastings.

MYSTERIES OF THE MALE MIND No.6

WHY DON'T FELLAS EVER NOTICE WHAT YOU'RE WEARING?

But — according to Bob — they do! And how!

Oh yeah — we fellas are quite observant. S'pose it comes from being in the boy scouts.

In fact we used to get a proficiency badge for being alert.

And we learnt all about the layered look keeping warm at camp.

When it comes to the bottom of it all there's not much we miss, honest!

—Cor! Look at them! You can tell they're padded by the lumps.

Nah! They're not stockings! Suspenders always make little bumps on the thighs.

Not much hope there! Knickers, tights — and vest!!! Look at all those bulges.

Cheeky! She couldn't even get a bus ticket under them!

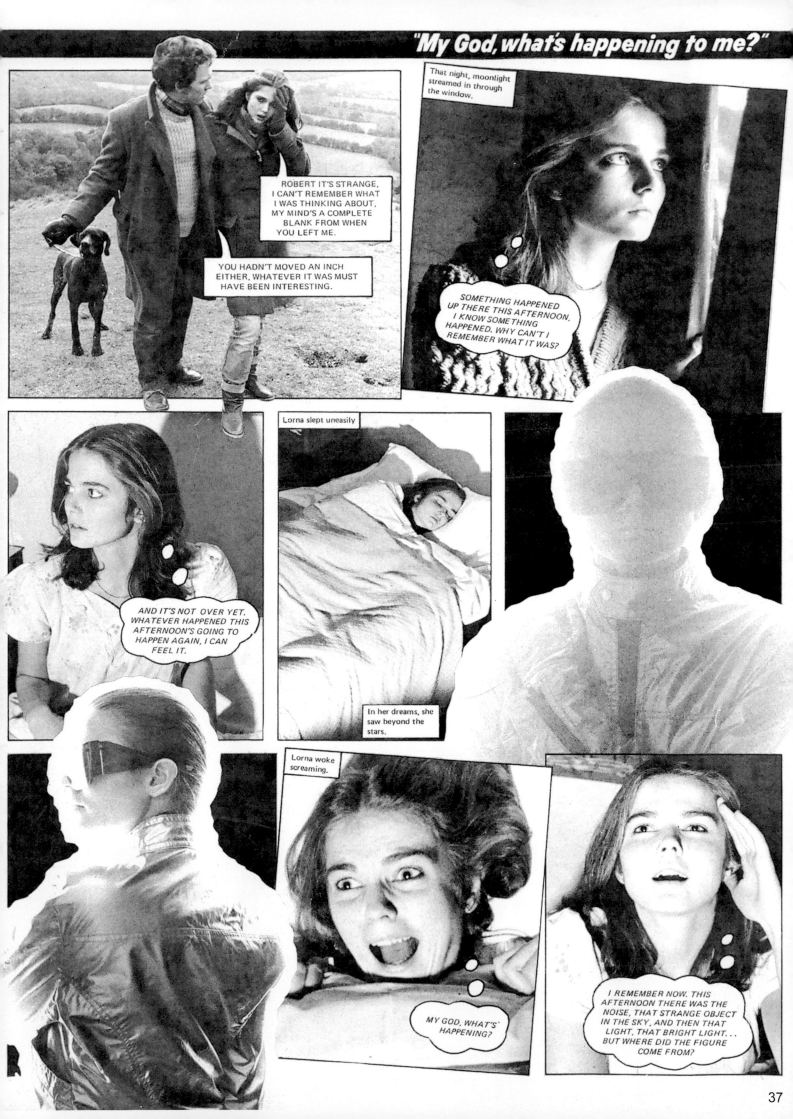

ROBERT IT'S STRANGE, I CAN'T REMEMBER WHAT I WAS THINKING ABOUT, MY MIND'S A COMPLETE BLANK FROM WHEN YOU LEFT ME.

YOU HADN'T MOVED AN INCH EITHER, WHATEVER IT WAS MUST HAVE BEEN INTERESTING.

That night, moonlight streamed in through the window.

SOMETHING HAPPENED UP THERE THIS AFTERNOON, I KNOW SOMETHING HAPPENED. WHY CAN'T I REMEMBER WHAT IT WAS?

AND IT'S NOT OVER YET. WHATEVER HAPPENED THIS AFTERNOON'S GOING TO HAPPEN AGAIN, I CAN FEEL IT.

Lorna slept uneasily

In her dreams, she saw beyond the stars.

Lorna woke screaming.

MY GOD, WHAT'S HAPPENING?

I REMEMBER NOW. THIS AFTERNOON THERE WAS THE NOISE, THAT STRANGE OBJECT IN THE SKY, AND THEN THAT LIGHT, THAT BRIGHT LIGHT... BUT WHERE DID THE FIGURE COME FROM?

COME ON LORNA YOU DON'T EXPECT ME TO BELIEVE YOU SAW A U.F.O., THEN FORGOT IT JUST LIKE THAT. YOU MUST HAVE IMAGINED IT.

I DID SEE SOME—THING ROBERT, BELIEVE ME!

KEEP YOUR VOICE DOWN, THERE'S NO NEED TO SHOUT. O.K. YOU SAW AN ODD SHAPE, THEN A BURST OF SUNLIGHT CAME THROUGH THE CLOUDS. I WOULDN'T EXACTLY CALL THAT FIRM EVIDENCE OF A MARTIAN INVASION FLEET.

I THOUGHT OF ALL PEOPLE, AT LEAST YOU'D BELIEVE ME.

LORNA, I WAS ON THE SAME HILLSIDE, WHY DIDN'T I SEE IT?

That night Lorna fell asleep in the chair by the curtain.

PERHAPS IT'S BECAUSE YOU DON'T WANT TO BELIEVE IT. I DO. I BELIEVE THERE'S SOME—THING OUT THERE, AND I BELIEVE THEY'LL COME BACK.

Again she dreamed of the figure in the silver suit.

Waking in the morning, she knew.

THAT'S THE SAME DREAM AGAIN. I THINK I KNOW WHAT IT MEANS NOW.

I'M GOING UP TO THE HILL. I'VE GOT TO FIND OUT ABOUT THE FIGURE. I KNOW THEY'LL COME BACK...

ALL I HAVE TO DO IS WAIT.

STAR GUY

2nd Time Lucky, Midge?

*"You betcha!"
says the likely lad
from Glasgow. 'Cos
this time around
he's going to make
it — or break
it . . .*

MY GUY
CHAPTER TWO

OUT OF THE DARKNESS

Carol thought she was alone–but a stranger was watching...

THAT'S ODD, I'M SURE I HEARD A CAR IN THE LANE.

STILL, THESE WILL BRIGHTEN UP THE HOUSE FOR A BIT.

I WONDER WHO COULD BE CALLING ON THE HOUSE? I DON'T OFTEN GET VISITORS OUT HERE

DAMN! IT WAS PROBABLY THE ELECTRICITY BOARD AND I'VE MISSED THEM.

Turn to page 80

POP
with Andy

MARTIN AND A CASE OF MISTAKEN IDENTITY!

Martin Gordon of Radio Stars was once standing at a bus stop when he saw his girlfriend go past hanging on the arm of another guy!

"I was fuming!" he said. "So I decided to follow. I chased them a long way, keeping a fair distance behind so they wouldn't spot me.

"I followed them down a couple of streets, in and out of some shops and on to a bus.

"I sat behind them for a while, but then I couldn't contain my anger any longer.

"I went up to their seat, tapped her on the shoulder and let out a stream of abuse!

"Then to my horror, I saw it wasn't my girlfriend — just someone who looked like her!

"I've never run so fast in my life!"

Ah well, Martin. Just imagine if she'd turned out to be Julie — you'd have run even faster!

DON'T BARK FOR ME, ARGENTINA!

When David Essex was rehearsing in 'Evita' he took his dog to the theatre with him. And she got stage struck!

"She was convinced she'd landed the star part!" said David. "She sat in the front row and wagged her tail.

"Then she leapt on stage to join in a crowd scene. She got so excited she kept barking and people tripped over her.

"In the end someone had to go out and buy a big bone to lure her offstage with!

"I found her later in the dressing room gazing into the mirror and looking very hurt.

"I had to give her loads of biscuits to make up for it!"

ROBYN'S LANDSCAPE SCRAPE!

Robyn Hitchcook of The Soft Boys thought he'd try his hand out as a painter recently.

"I've always liked painting," he said, "so the other day I went out into the country to do some.

"I'd just set my easel up in this field and sat down when a cow wandered up to watch me.

"Before I could finish my masterpiece, the cow chomped a big chunk out of the canvas!

"I made a grab for it, overbalanced and landed splat in a cow pat!

"Bet Picasso never had that sort of trouble . . ."

STARS

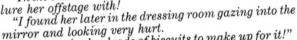

Your stars for week beginning Sat. Sept. 16th

	Elton — **ARIES** (Mar. 21st – Apr. 20th)	Martin Gordon — **TAURUS** (Apr. 21st. –May 22nd)	Suzi Quatro — **GEMINI** (May 23rd – June 21st)	Brian May — **CANCER** (Jun 22nd – July 22nd)	Oliver Tobias — **LEO** (July 23rd – Aug 22nd)	Knox (Vibrators) — **VIRGO** (Aug 23rd – Sep 22nd)
SAT & SUN	Your social life just couldn't be better at the moment. Make the most of it!	You're asking too much of people – try not to be so demanding for a change.	You can't be everywhere at once. So stop rushing around. Be calm!	You've got a big chance coming up – make sure you don't mess things up!	You're stuck in a rut — now's the time to make a move and do something different.	Don't put off what can be done now. You'll only regret it if you do.
MON	Parents might seem short-tempered. Bear with them.	Feeling fed-up? Well don't worry. It won't last long.	You hear from someone who you thought had forgotten you.	You think you're being got at but it's all in your head.	If that fella asks you out — make sure you accept.	We all know it's sensible to save – but it's great to splash out!
TUES	That fella really does like you — he's not bluffing this time!	At last that fella rings you up. Try to play it cool.	Someone close to you is feeling miserable — be sympathetic.	You've got to stop your friend making a big mistake.	Someone's being bitchy but it's really only jealousy.	There's an illness in the family – but it's nothing serious.
WEDS	Money could be a bit short — don't be extravagant.	It's time to splash out and buy some new clothes.	You can't afford that dress — and you know it!	Need something new to wear? Then make it!	There's an outing coming up — make sure you don't miss out.	You lose something that you value highly – keep searching.
THURS	There's a letter on its way to you. Expect a surprise!	Everyone's having a good laugh at your expense. Never mind.	You're leading that fella a dog's life. You'll regret it.	It seems Mr Right is on your doorstep – but who is he?	Feeling ill? — Maybe you need a break. Go and visit a friend.	Stop questioning your fella - it'll only cause arguments.
FRI	Trouble at work? Your attention's wandering. Take care!	Don't gossip. It'll all get back to you in the end.	You forget someone's birthday and they're really hurt.	There's party coming up and all your mates will be there.	Don't forget to reply to that letter. It's important.	Don't believe everything you hear – there's nothing in rumours

STARS FOR YOU!

'BRITAIN'S STICKY!' SAY THE DICKIES

American punk group The Dickies couldn't wait to come to Britain to play some gigs.

After all, the band had only got together in the first place after being inspired by British punks.

"We saw The Damned when they were in America," Dan Lee told us. "We loved them, and decided to form a group to play that sort of music."

"Yeah, so we couldn't wait to come over to Britain," added Billy Club. "We were sure audiences here would love us.

"Unfortunately they did!"

Unfortunately?

"Well, they loved us so much," explained Billy, "they showed their appreciation by spitting all over us!

"We were covered in the stuff! Audiences in the States just don't do that!

"We love British fans — but next time we'll wear macs!"

MG MG MG

Maybe the sight of Suzi Quatro in tight leather trousers playing the part of 'Leather' in Happy Days' doesn't do much for your fella.

But guess who they wanted to do the part in the first place? Would ya believe Debbie Harry! In the end they thought she was too old. Boy she's the kind of older woman I could learn to like . . !

MG MG MG

David Soul's just changed his phone number for the fourth time. Every time he switches it he gets a few months rest before numerous young ladies start ringing and making suggestions to him (Own up Julie — that's why the office phone bill was so high . . .)

MG MG MG

Bianca Jagger reckons that Mick likes intelligent women, but that he doesn't feel 'safe' with them — so he hangs around with dumb ones! If we didn't know better, we'd think she was being bitchy about Jerry Hall!

MG MG MG

Sylvester Stallone, star of 'Rocky' is thinking over an offer to play Elvis in a new film. There's just one little snag for Sylvester — he can't sing a note!

BEEN HERE BEFORE?

JOHN'S SECRET JOB!

John Gregg was born on November 3rd which makes his star sign Scorpio.

This means he's highly imaginative, and has strong, powerful emotions. He feels things deeply.

He likes to keep his feelings to himself, though, because he has a love of secrets.

He has an enormous amount of energy and believes in living life to the full.

He's the same in love, and puts everything into a relationship. But he can be extremely jealous — even if he has no real reason to be.

In a previous existence he may have been a psychiatrist living 50 years ago. He loved that job, 'cos he got to know lots of other people's secrets!

This time round there's one thing that isn't a secret: John's gorgeous looks will take him right to the top!

FREE AND EASY!
BAG SOME BARRY!

Barry Manilow fans, here's a chance to get a double helping of him!

Barry's got a new single out, and it's a double 'A' side. One side is a song called 'Somewhere In the Night' which is a powerful ballad. On the other there's a great disco number called 'Copacabana'.

To win a copy write and tell us the title of Barry's last single. First 20 to get it right, get a freebie!

POP STARS

Brian Connelly	Chris Norman	Jeff Philipps	Tim Matheson	John Travolta	Dennis Waterman	
LIBRA *(Sep 23rd - Oct 22nd)*	**SCORPIO** *(Oct 23rd - Nov 21st)*	**SAGITTARIUS** *(Nov 22nd - Dec 22nd)*	**CAPRICORN** *(Dec 23rd - Jan 20th)*	**AQUARIUS** *(Jan 21st - Feb 19th)*	**PISCES** *(Feb 20th - Mar 20th)*	
Leave that fella alone — he's not yours and he doesn't really want to be either.	A quiet weekend. But don't worry, things will soon brighten up.	Feeling confused? Then shut yourself away from everyone and think things out.	A fella you meet on Saturday isn't all that he makes himself out to be.	Something's bothering you. It's time you confided in a close friend.	That job you wrote after could be yours - if you play your cards right!	**SAT & SUN**
You're doing well at work and heading for a rise.	There's a family wedding coming up soon.	You feel annoyed — but don't start any arguments.	A small child is annoying you – be patient.	You've made your decision. Now be sure to stick to it.	That joke has gone too far. It's time to tell the truth.	**MON**
Luck is certainly running for you at the moment.	It's time to settle any debts that you may have.	Your best friend splits up with her fella. Be kind.	Trouble at home won't last long, so don't let it worry you.	You're working hard be sure not to over-do things.	Don't argue with your Mum. You'll only upset her.	**TUES**
Feeling bored? Then join a club and make more friends.	Someone is bossing you around who has no right to.	Socially you're bored — try going to a few different places	It looks like your romance is heading for the rocks.	Don't wait in for that phone call — it's not worth it.	Someone's spreading rumours about you. Don't worry.	**WEDS**
Entered any competitions lately? Then you could be lucky.	Don't eavesdrop - you could end up feeling hurt.	It's no use kidding yourself — you and your fella should split.	Your career is in the balance. Careful what you say.	It seems you've got a secret admirer — lucky you.	You'll meet a new fella and you'll be mad about him.	**THURS**
Your Mum's feeling depressed. Help her out.	That bargain isn't a good buy at all. Never mind.	Experiment with your make-up for a new look.	Ill health has been bothering you – go and see your doctor.	There's a flaming row — and it's over you! Cool it down!	It's time you shed a few pounds. Go on a diet.	**FRI**

45

I'M TOO SHY

Name: Julie Briscoll
Problem: Julie's so sure Paul likes her. But so far, they've never spoken!

I hadn't really noticed Paul at school. Then one day . . .

EXCUSE ME. I DON'T WANT TO BREAK THIS UP, BUT I'VE GOT A LESSON TO GO TO!

It's funny how you can suddenly click with somone.

It seemed such a small incident, but it set me thinking.

WHO WAS THAT? I'VE SEEN HIM AROUND, BUT I DON'T KNOW HIS NAME.

THAT'S PAUL HARRISON. . . WHY?

I'd never had a proper boyfriend and I wasn't too sure what to do next.

ARE YOU INTERESTED THEN?

NO, NOT REALLY. SEE YOU LATER, LAURIE.

But I was interested — very!

From then on, I began to notice him more and more.

He seemed so warm and friendly.

Then I found out from a friend that he wasn't going out with anyone . . .

. . . so I could always hope.

I always looked for any signs of hope.

'SAW PAUL TODAY. HE SMILED AGAIN. HE CAME OUT OF THE SIXTH FORM BLOCK AND WALKED PAST ME. I REALLY LIKE HIM. . .'

And every time he passed me, I couldn't stop my heart from skipping a few beats.

Some days, if I hadn't seen him anywhere . . .

JULIE, WHAT ARE YOU DOING HANGING AROUND HERE? AREN'T YOU COMING TO DINNER?

ER . . . I'LL BE ALONG IN A MINUTE, YOU GO ON AHEAD.

. . . I'd hang around waiting for him to turn up.

PAUL'S GOT A MATHS LESSON JUST DOWN THE CORRIDOR, SO HE'LL HAVE TO COME THIS WAY!

I was so sure he liked me, because he always smiled at me when we met . . .

. . . but I was too scared to do or say anything, just in case I got it all wrong.

WIN A WEEK IN THE STATES!

FANTASTIC FREE! LEIF GARRETT COMPETITION

'MEET ME IN HOLLYWOOD!'
says LEIF

YES, that's the incredible top prize in My Guy's first ever competition! You'll meet Leif, America's hottest young superstar. You'll get to know him from the inside, see him in his private, intimate moments, and share all the behind-the-scenes excitement of his life! Imagine – a week in the beautiful Golden State of California, expenses paid! And you can take a friend with you – or even your mum! – and have yourselves the holiday you've always dreamed of, 7 days of fun, fun, fun! Just think of the sunshine, the beaches, the palm trees waving in the warm Pacific winds . . . the fun of Disneyland . . . the company of Leif in the showbiz capital of the world . . . it really is THE PRIZE OF A LIFETIME.

★ ★

1st PRIZE: **A WEEK IN HOLLYWOOD, ALL EXPENSES PAID!**

2nd PRIZES: **20 TOP QUALITY SKATEBOARDS AND SKATEBOARD KITS!**

3rd PRIZES: **100 AUTOGRAPHED LEIF GARRETT ALBUMS!**

4th PRIZES: **250 BEAUTIFUL AUTOGRAPHED LEIF GARRETT POSTERS!**

★ ★

HOW DO YOU ENTER?

Listed are just eight of the many things which have helped to make Leif Garrett a superstar in America. How do you rate them as being likely to contribute to his success in this country?

Write the key letters of the eight factors — in ink, pen or ballpoint — in order of choice on your entry coupon. For example, if you consider that his looks will appeal to British audiences more so than any of the other factors, put B in the first space; the letter of your next choice goes against 2nd, and so on for all eight.

Complete the coupon with your own full name and address, and post in a sealed envelope to: LEIF'S HOLLYWOOD COMPETITION, MY GUY, 55 EWER STREET, LONDON, SE99 6YP, to arrive not later than Monday 3rd April, 1978. **IMPORTANT** Before sealing, copy out — on the outside of the envelope — the eight key letters in exactly the same order as they appear on your completed coupon. Do not enclose any correspondence or matter other than the coupon.

HOW IMPORTANT ARE THESE QUALITIES OF LEIF GARRETT?

A. His individual voice and style of singing.
B. His great looks.
C. He's not 'big-headed'.
D. His choice of lovely songs.
E. His professionalism on stage.
J. His clothes and style

K. He's got all round talent.
L. His sexy body.

POST TO: LEIF'S HOLLYWOOD COMPETITION, 55 EWER STREET, LONDON SE99 6YP.

My order of choice for the eight reasons is listed on the right.
I agree to the rules as legally binding.

Closing date: April 3rd, 1978.

NAME _____ AGE _____

ADDRESS _____

_____

_____

1	
2	
3	
4	
5	
6	
7	
8	

REMEMBER! Somebody's going to meet Leif in Hollywood. Why shouldn't it be YOU?!

MY GUY
LEIF GARRETT

Cute American whizz-kid
— see him soon in
'Skateboard!'

49

MY GUY PHOTO STORY

SISTER BLACKMAIL!

With the pictures she had, Deidre was ready to make her sister's life hell!

GET AWAY FROM ME, YOU BITCH!

MORNING, SISTER DEAR — AND HOW ARE WE TODAY?

HERE SHE COMES, IN MY JUMPER AND MY BOOTS!

I was itching to tear her hair out by the roots — but I knew I couldn't . . .

YOU'D BETTER LEAVE OFF CALLING ME NAMES, JUNE. YOU WOULDN'T WANT ANYONE TO SEE MY PHOTO ALBUM WOULD YOU?

YOU KNOW DAMN WELL I WOULDN'T!

WELL, WATCH IT! NOW — HOW WOULD YOU LIKE TO COME OUT FOR A WALK WITH ME, THERE'S SOMETHING I'D LIKE TO SHOW YOU . . . .

Now turn to page 88 to find out how the story ends

Today Girl

Name: Sally. Age: 16
Lives at: Petersham, Surrey
At the moment: Student

Sally is one of the Today Girls

She's still at school, but has loads of spare-time interests, and a big ambition — to dance, one day, in a group like the Young Generation.

Music is another big thing with Sally. Modern, of course — with Elton John, Rod Stewart and The Eagles sharing top place. And so is keeping fit, for the suppleness that's a must for a dancer. So Sally plays squash a lot, and goes swimming too. Which all means lots of rushing around, plenty of hard work at her evening dance classes — and at her age, a natural tendency to oily skin, with its risk of clogged pores and blackheads.

That's why Sally uses Deep Cleansing Tonic, because it makes her face really clean and fresh, and its mild medication helps keep spots at bay. But she also likes its fresh, non-medicated smell — important when her regular boyfriend calls around.

There are millions of girls like Sally, living their lives their own way, with their own ideas, their own dreams. If you would like to feature as a "Today Girl" take a look at the info below . . .

Deep Cleansing Tonic
medicated
for oily skins

DDD ✚ Deep Cleansing Tonic

chosen by Today Girls

be a TODAY GIRL - here's how!

Just send us some basic details about yourself, plus a photo, (sorry we can't send it back) and a Deep Cleansing Tonic label and you could end up on this page, and have £50 to spend any way you want.

Write to: "Today Girl", DDD Limited, 94 Rickmansworth Road, Watford, Herts. WD1 7JJ.

Paul Came Back Today

Lynn lived for the day when the fair came back to town. Because Paul came with it . . .

"DID you know the fair's back in town?" My mate Ellie said. "Over on Smithy's Common."

And in my heart a dream came back to life.

"Oh is it?" I said as casually as I could.

There were grey clouds in the sky, but they seemed to vanish. The sun was shining again. The fair was here. Paul had come back to me, just like he promised he would . . .

How long was it since I'd seen him? Must be about six months. But it seemed longer.

Every day without Paul had been a misery for me.

I could remember the very first time I'd seen him. The special magic of that night we'd met at the fair, with its bright lights and gay music . . .

I'd gone there with Mike, my steady fella. We wandered through the fair together, trying the different rides.

But Mike wasn't enjoying himself.

"Dunno why you wanted to come here, Lynn," he said.

I didn't answer him. The fairground music was playing in my ears, the bright lights were flashing all around me, and I felt lost in a magic world.

Then I sensed somebody was watching me, and saw Paul for the first time.

He was in charge of one of the merry-go-rounds . . . a whirling stampede of wooden ponies, with bright manes and painted bodies. And he was watching me.

STARING

For a minute we just kept staring at each other across the fairground, like we were waiting to see who would look away first. It was me who finally dropped my eyes, but I'd had time enough to grab a quick impression of a tall boy with dark hair and darker eyes, eyes that I knew were still watching me.

"What's up?" Mike asked, looking at me curiously. "You've gone quiet."

"Nothing," I said, thinking of the boy at the merry-go-round. The boy who'd sent my heart beating crazily just by looking at me. "I'm a bit browned off with this place. Let's go."

Mike didn't argue.

He walked me home and I told him I was going to have an

A MY GUY HEART TOUCHING STORY

early night 'cos I had a headache. But once I got indoors I just sat there, thinking about the way the boy at the fairground had looked at me. I knew the fair would be open for another few hours. Without giving myself time to think, I hurried back.

Paul saw me coming long before I reached his merry-go-round. There was a grin on his face as he helped me onto one of the wooden ponies, his eyes laughing.

I watched him make his way around the moving platform collecting money from the other riders. He moved easily, sure-footed as a cat. And his eyes kept drifting back to me . . .

When the music ended and the wooden ponies stopped, Paul came over to me.

"What happened to the guy you were with?" he said.

"He's gone home."

"Good." Paul smiled at me, his dark eyes seemed as if they were full of hidden depths. "My relief takes over in ten minutes. Stick around, kid, and I'll show you all the fun of the fair . . ."

That was the way it started for us. That night, Paul and I drifted around the fair together as if we'd known each other for years. Paul told me all about his job.

"It's terrific," he said. "Never staying too long in one place, always on the move. Makes life like one great big merry-go-round."

"How long will you be here?" I asked him quietly.

"Three weeks, maybe four." He took my hands and looked down at me with those dark eyes. "That's long enough, isn't it? To get to know each other . . ."

When he kissed me, the music of the fair was singing in my ears, and out of the corner of my eye I could see the painted ponies whirling past.

There was magic all around me, but Paul was the best magic . . .

Every day we were together.

Paul was different from any boy I'd ever known before. There was a strange kind of excitement about him, maybe because of the fair.

"I was born into it," he told me. "Never wanted to do anything else."

"Don't you ever feel you'd like to settle down?" I asked him once. "Don't you want the merry-go-round to stop?"

"Maybe," he said. "One day . . ." And he kissed me then, and told me how much he loved me.

Mike didn't mean anything to me anymore. I'd told him we were through.

He didn't understand what I saw in Paul. Maybe nobody

did. They didn't know the way he could make my heart sing just by touching my hand, or running his fingers through my hair. Paul was the only boy in the world for me. But I always knew one day he would leave, when the fair moved on.

On that last night I cried.

"I don't want you to go, Paul," I whispered. "I love you!" He kissed my cheek.

PROMISE

"I'll be back, Lynn. One day the fair will come back here again, and I'll be with it."

"You promise?" I asked, my eyes filled with tears. "You won't forget me, Paul?"

"I promise," he whispered. "I'll come back to you, Lynn."

And now the fair was here, and Paul would be with it.

He hadn't written to me, but I'd never expected that. Paul wasn't the sort of boy to write letters. But that didn't matter. Nothing mattered except that he'd come back to me.

I hurried towards Smithy's Common and even before I reached it I heard the sound of the fairground music, that had haunted my dreams.

And there stood the fair.

The lights were sparkling and the merry-go-round whirling. The painted ponies still raced round in their mad stampede.

I ran forward, my eyes searching for Paul's figure. Then I saw him, standing by the merry-go-round, his eyes laughing as they'd been doing on that first night we met. He was helping a girl onto one of the wooden ponies, a laughing girl, slim and pretty. His arm was round her shoulder and he was smiling down at her.

"My relief takes over in ten minutes," I heard him tell her. "Stick around kid, and I'll show you all the fun of the fair . . ."

For a while I stood and watched, seeing the way he was laughing down into the girl's eyes, as he had once done with me. The ponies came to a halt and Paul put his arm round the girl and led her away.

Then I turned away, blinded by tears, knowing that even if Paul saw me he probably wouldn't be able to remember my name.

Love was just a merry-go-round to him, one that would never stop turning. Every time one girl got off, there was another to take her place. And I'd had my turn.

I walked away from the fair, my eyes blinded by the brightness of the lights and my own tears.

All around there was music and laughter and behind me the painted ponies turned on and on in their mad dance.

A TOUCH OF CLASS!

Classy clobber needn't cost a bomb! Do a bit of homework and scout around your local high street — you'll get full marks for style . . !

BOB

Left: Printed cream skirt available in other colourways price £11.99, shirt £7.99. Both from Top Shop branches. Knitted cardigan £5.99 sizes 12-16 and matching shawl £3.99 from all larger branches of Boots. Shoes by Dolcis £12.99. **Right:** Skirt from Top Shop price £9.99. Cream shirt price £6.99 from major Littlewoods stores. Hand-knitted cardigan £10.95 and slipover £7.99 from 'Just-In' departments in most Debenham stores. Shoes by Curtess £9.99. Socks by Sunarama.

Left: Trousers £8.99, waistcoat £4.99, shirt £7.99 from Marks & Spencer's Teen Range. Hat by Boots £4.95. Boots from Littlewoods £18.99. **Right:** Sweater £11.99, cords £8.99 from British Home Stores. Belt 99p, satchel £4.95 by Boots. Boots from British Home Stores £9.99.

Left: Skirt from Top Shop £11.99. Jumper from Tesco's Home 'N' Wear depts price £6.99. Scarf from Littlewoods £1.99. Shoes by Dolcis, £12.99. **Right:** Jacket £14.99 and cords £5.99 from Tesco's Home 'N' Wear depts. Shirt from Top Shop £7.99. Shoes by Saxone £14.99.

Left: Shetland trousers £9.99 and waistcoat £6.50 from most branches of Littlewoods. Shirt from Top Shop £7.99. Boots from major branches of Littlewoods, £18.99. **Right:** Tweed skirt £7.99, jacket with elbow patches £15.99 from all branches of Littlewoods.

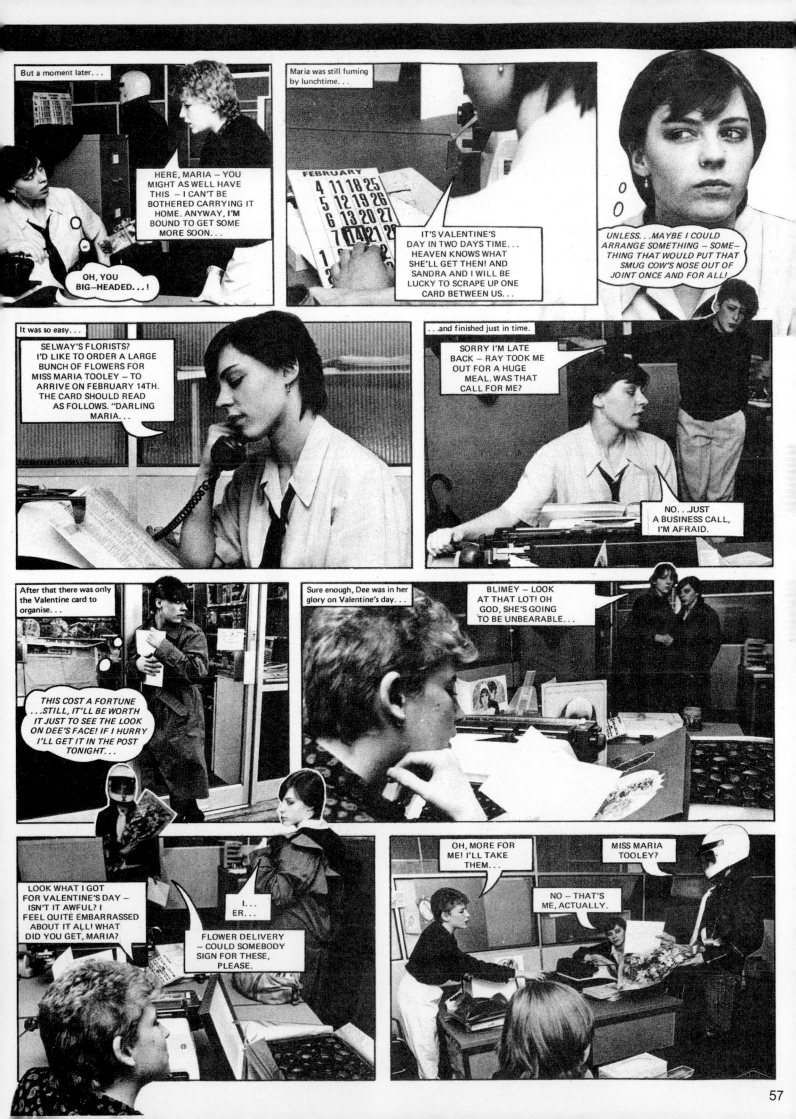

Welcome to DAFT CITY!

IS THAT A FACT?

Daft by name and daft by nature, that's this page. All the best rumours start here! Plus — weird stories and funny tales that'll have you in fits! Promise!

Angel with a bedpan??

I've heard that Cheryl Ladd really wanted to be a nurse, but that her Dad was a film star and forced her into acting, even though she just hates it!
Lynn, Derby.

This is a new one! Cheryl is married to David Ladd, whose Dad, Alan, was a big film star. And she's always wanted to be an actress, which is why she struggled in small parts before becoming one of the Angels. As for the nursing . . . funny, but soon as he heard it, Bob went down with a cold!!!

BIG, WET WINKLER!

My Grannie says that Henry Winkler isn't so tough. She reckons she's heard that he's scared of the dark and has to sleep with the light on. Is this true? 'Cos sometimes she imagines things and I never know when she has!
Debbie, Hastings

*So that's where all these daft rumours have come from! Your Gran's just gotta cut this out, 'cos it's hard work checking 'em all. Henry isn't scared of the dark, but there's one thing he's terrified of – being known as 'The Fonz' for the rest of his life! That's why, right now, he's steering clear of 'Happy Days' and trying to make his own name more famous. We've heard that the next fan who asks for **that** autograph, is going to find out just how tough Fonzie can be!*

RAT ON THE SKIDS?

I read somewhere that Rat Scabies has quit the music business since he left the Damned and is now working as a skateboard salesman. Tell me it can't be true, 'cos I think he's the greatest drummer out!
Gill, Torquay.

It WAS true. After leaving The Damned, poor ol' Rat did sell skateboards for a while to make ends meet. But the latest news is that he's putting a new band together and with luck you'll be hearing them soon.

UNDIE OFFER!

IF you're into underwear you're in good company. Spike Milligan (strange man) recently put in a bid of £50 for a pair of Queen Victoria's knickers. (Hope she washed 'em first!) Wonder what Rod Stewart would get for these then? Bidding starts at 70p and works downwards — how far, we're not saying! All enquiries, in a plain brown envelope please, should be addressed to Julie's Bottom Drawer! (PS Marty Feldman got Victoria's knicks for £160!!)

MIAOW!

WHO'S this flying the flag for Britain then? None other than Peter Powell. Well, Peter, we know you're working for that good old British institution the Beeb now, but don't you think you've taken it a bit too far? It's enough to make your hair curl – oh, it has! Shouldn't you have had your chest done to match? How low can you get? Not much lower by the state of that zip. Cor! If the BBC got hold of this one they'd have you on the first flight to Luxembourg! Still, they could always re-title your Sunday morning spot 'What There Is To See' instead of Hear . . .

Anyway, we're prepared to make a deal. No more pics like this and we won't show it to your new bosses. Done!

ASK A STOOPID QUESTION...

We put the Jam's Bruce Foxton in the hot seat, and asked him the daftest things ever! He grunted, he gasped, he groaned — then he spilled the beans!

1. What's your fave flavour chewing gum?
"Wrigleys Doublemint."

2. What's your usual pick-up line?
"I've been going steady so long, I've forgotten 'em!"

3. What do girls wear in your dreams?
"Very little . . ."

4. Who would you most hate to meet?
"I've already met him! But I better not say who it is!"

5. When you undress, what d'you take off last?
"My socks. I look very sexy in 'em!"

6. Have you got any nasty secrets?
"Nope — I told everyone 'em all — so they're not secrets anymore."

7. Are you scared of creepy-crawlies?
"Yeah, I don't like spiders."

8. When you can't sleep, d'you count sheep ... or what?
"What!"

9. What's the last thing you do at night?
"Turn off my electric blanket, of course!"

10. D'you have a Basil Brush pin-up?
"Nope, but I bought my girlfriend one!"

WHAT MAKES A GORGEOUS

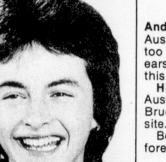

● Apart from tickling his ribs, probably quite a few things, like the sight of you in your curlers and facepack or seeing a size fourteen bum squeezed into a pair of size ten jeans . . . (Ho, ho!). But seriously(!), get a laugh out of a guy and you're half-way home!

So, to find out what made the tastiest guys around split their sides, we asked 'em to tell us their favourite jokes. (Asking for trouble, innit?) And now you know how to get 'em helpless (with laughter), dontcha . . . !

I'M BRUCE—FLY ME!

Andy Gibb has a store of rude Aussie tales but they were all too unclean for your tender ears! Then he remembered this one . . .

His joke: This thick Australian yob, let's call him Bruce, signed on at a building site.

Being such a bullhead, the foreman told another guy, a

real intelligent, ex-pilot, to keep an eye on him.

Anyway, Bruce and the ex-pilot were sent to work on the ninth floor of a block of flats.

Ten minutes later, the foreman saw Bruce leap off the scaffolding and land, splat, in the concrete below, dead as a wombat.

So the foreman rushed up to the ex-pilot.

'What the **** happened?!' he yelled.

And the guy replied, casually. 'Aw, I just told him I used to fly Wellingtons during the war.!'

Well, it's clean!

BOOBY TRAPS!

The best joke **Martin Gordon's** ever seen or heard is an episode of *Crossroads!* But, apart from wisecracks from Sandy Richardson anything's good for a giggle to him, 'specially if it's female! So here's one of his favourites!

His joke: Why is a bra like a sheepdog? 'Cos it rounds 'em up an' points 'em in the right direction!

MYSTERIES OF THE MALE MIND No.8

Yup! It's wonderboy Bob – the fella with all the answers . . .

WHY DO FELLAS' CARS ALWAYS CONK OUT IN COUNTRY LANES?

IRISH EYES ARE LAUGHING!

Doesn't take much to set **Ian Mitchell** off! Practically anything'll get him going . . . And, being Irish he's got a host of funnies from the Emerald Isles!

His jokes: This Irishman entered the Indianapolis 500 race. He'd have done all right if he hadn't had 32 pit stops — one for petrol and 31 to ask the way!

And . . . What happened to the Irish firing squad?

Formed a circle and shot each other!

Those country lanes play havoc on your suspension . . .

— *Sorry luv — looks like me big end's gone again —*

And cranking up ya shaft in front of a bird ain't too romantic.

— *Hmm, looks bad. Better go and call a garage —*

I always believe in consulting the experts . . .

(Three minutes later) — Fella suggested we bounce about in the back!

S'funny how they always know best!

(Three hours later.) Success at last. That got her going! —

UY GIGGLE?

SILLY ASS!

Most humour gets **David Essex** rolling in the aisles — tho' that's usually where he gets his audience dancing!

His joke: This man went into a bar and ordered a drink.

'Pint of bitter, please, donkey,' he said to the barman.

The barman pulled a pint and handed it over.

'Thanks, donkey,' said the man.

A while later, he bought another pint — and again called the barman donkey.

When he sat down, another guy called the barman over and said, curiously,

'Why's he keep calling you donkey?'

'I dunno' he replied.

'He-haw, he-haw, he-halways calls me that.'!

GORILLA AN' BEAR IT!

Biggest joke **Leif Garrett** could think of was being mistaken for Brigitte Bardot — from behind! But after that, this one got him going!

His joke: This guy kept a gorilla in a cage in his lounge. He told everyone it was OK just so long as nobody touched it. Well, that really bugged one of his friends.

So, one night, he sneaked into the guy's lounge, crept up to the gorilla's cage, and touched him.

Immediately, the gorilla went wild, smashed its way out of the cage and started after the guy who was way down the avenue by then and up a lampost.

When the gorilla made it to the top, he reached out a massive paw, touched his arm and said (wait for it), 'You're it.'!

YELLOW PERIL!

Took **Paul Jackson** some time to think of a good giggle, in the end he dragged out this old chestnut!

His joke: What's yellow, yodels and swings from tree to tree?

Tarzipan!

VERY ANDY!

You can't call Andy gorgeous so he's nothing much to giggle about. Still, his piccie's enough to give you a laugh!

His joke: How d'ya make rhubarb wine? Hit it with a stick! (Works on Julie too!)

WHAT GETS YOU GIGGLING?

Reckon you can do better han this lovely lot? If ya do, rite and tell us!

Send your favourite joke to: My Guy Giggles, 21st Floor, King's Reach Tower, Stamford Street, London SE1 9LS. First prize (joke): A cand-

lelit dinner for two at The Greasy Spoon, Cricklewood.

Second prize (joke): A weekend at The Greasy Spoon, Cricklewood.

And we'll publish the best of the bunch, your jokes that is, at £2 a throw!

SECOND TIME LUCKY?

STAR STORY

'Not many people get the chance to be a star once, let alone twice!'

When a former teenybop star gets together with an ex-Sex Pistol to form a band, it's bound to be a strange mixture! But is it the right mixture? Midge Ure told us how he rated his chances of making it . . . second time around!

"The trouble with Slik," said Midge, "was that we were incredibly successful just after the Rollers. Everybody saw us as a follow up to them.

"But the only thing we really had in common with them was being Scottish! We considered ourselves good musicians who could play good music, but people just wanted us to parade in our baseball gear and play rubbish.

"We got fed up with the whole thing. We weren't recording, we were just playing dates in Europe. That made us plenty of money, but we knew we were just living off the old Slik reputation.

"So we all decided the best thing would be to split up, and try to make it with other bands.

"I sat around in Glasgow feeling wasted. I missed being in the limelight. I wanted to get back there.

"The problem was how! Then Glen Matlock phoned me up and asked me to join the Rich Kids.

"I had to think about it very hard. There I was up in Glasgow, with a home and a bit of money left. And they were down in London — squatting!

"So it was a big risk.

"But nothing else was happening, so I decided to accept.

"When I got to London, the other lads were a bit wary of me at first.

"I think they were a bit put off by the pop star image.

"But when we started playing together, suddenly we all knew it was gonna be all right.

"We made a great band! And in no time at all, loads of record companies were sniffing around wanting to sign us up!

"Course, a few months later our first single was in the charts!

"I'll be really upset if this band doesn't make it, 'cos I think it deserves to.

"Not many people get the chance to be a star once, let alone twice. So this time I'm determined to make it work.

"But if it doesn't, I'll try again.

"Music has been my life ever since I can remember, and I can't imagine ever giving it up.

"Not for another twenty years, anyway!"

Stay with it Midge! 'Cos us girls are gonna stay with you. Even if it does take a third time!

OLIVER TOBIAS

Remember him in *Luke's Kingdom*? All we can say, Oliver is ... can we please have some more ?!

64

MY GUY COMPLETE LOVE STORY

STRANGER ON THE SHORE

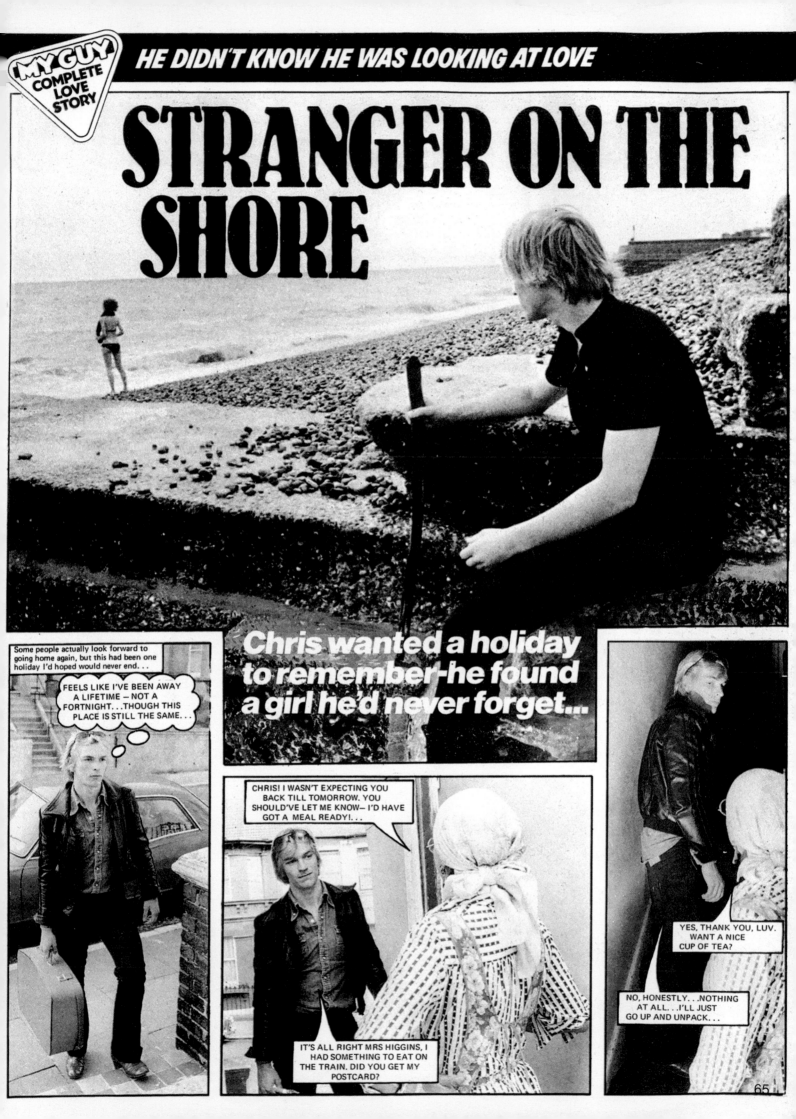

Chris wanted a holiday to remember—he found a girl he'd never forget...

Some people actually look forward to going home again, but this had been one holiday I'd hoped would never end. . .

FEELS LIKE I'VE BEEN AWAY A LIFETIME — NOT A FORTNIGHT. . .THOUGH THIS PLACE IS STILL THE SAME. . .

CHRIS! I WASN'T EXPECTING YOU BACK TILL TOMORROW. YOU SHOULD'VE LET ME KNOW— I'D HAVE GOT A MEAL READY!. . .

IT'S ALL RIGHT MRS HIGGINS, I HAD SOMETHING TO EAT ON THE TRAIN. DID YOU GET MY POSTCARD?

YES, THANK YOU, LUV. WANT A NICE CUP OF TEA?

NO, HONESTLY. . .NOTHING AT ALL. . .I'LL JUST GO UP AND UNPACK. . .

I KNOW SHE MEANS WELL, BUT ALL I NEED. . . IS TO BE ALONE. . .

I S'POSE I MIGHT AS WELL UNPACK. . .THE HOLIDAY IS OVER AFTER ALL. . .THOUGH IT'S ONE I'LL NEVER FORGET-EVER. . .

HOW CAN I, SUZY. . . WHEN THERE'S SO MUCH TO REMIND ME. . .?

LIKE THIS SHELL YOU GAVE ME. . .YOU SAID I'D ONLY HAVE TO HOLD IT AND YOU'D BE WITH ME AGAIN. . .

The holiday had started so badly. . .

GOD, WHAT A DUMP! IF I'D KNOWN THIS PLACE WAS SO DEAD I'D NEVER HAVE COME HERE. . . THERE'S NOT A SOUL ON THIS BEACH UNDER FIFTY. . .

EXCEPT THAT GIRL OVER THERE. . . AND SHE'S BEAUTIFUL!. . .AND WOULDN'T LOOK TWICE AT ME. . .

But I was wrong, wasn't I, Suzy. . .

HEY, HANG ON, YOU'VE LEFT YOUR RING BEHIND!

WH-WHAT? OH, DID I?

HERE, I'LL PUT IT ON FOR YOU!

N-NO. . .IT DOESN'T GO ON THAT FINGER. . .IT'S LUCKY YOU NOTICED, I DON'T KNOW WHAT I'D HAVE DONE IF I'D LOST IT!

LET ME BUY YOU A COFFEE TO SAY THANK-YOU!

GREAT! MY NAME'S CHRIS BY THE WAY

I didn't know if I'd make it to the cafe — my legs felt like jelly!

But I did — somehow! She told me her name was Suzy. . .

WHAT MADE YOU COME TO A DEAD PLACE LIKE THIS, SUZY?

OH, I'M HERE FOR THE SUMMER. . .ER . . .I'M LOOKING AFTER A, ER. . . RELATIVE WHO'S BEEN ILL, BUT I DON'T KNOW ANYONE HERE. . . PERHAPS WE COULD MEET FOR A SWIM ONE DAY?

NO — I MEAN, I'D LOVE TO... BUT I CAN'T SWIM! THAT MUST SOUND PRETTY STUPID TO YOU...

I HAVE TO GO NOW — BUT I'LL SEE YOU BY THE PIER FOR A SWIMMING LESSON, OKAY?

AS LONG AS YOU'LL LET ME TAKE YOU OUT AFTERWARDS...

OF COURSE IT DOESN'T! BUT YOU OUGHT TO HAVE A GO — I DON'T MIND HELPING YOU, — WE COULD HAVE A LESSON TOMORROW IF YOU LIKE!

I was still sitting there thinking about her when I saw her again. I nearly rushed after her — but she wasn't alone...

I couldn't wait to see her again! Next day, I was there hours early!

I BET SHE WON'T COME... I BET SHE'S FORGOTTEN ME ALREADY...

THAT MUST BE THE SICK RELATIVE SUZY'S LOOKING AFTER...IT'S PROBABLY HER FATHER...LOOKS AS IF IT COULD BE. WONDER WHY SHE DIDN'T INTRODUCE US?

MAYBE HE DOESN'T APPROVE OF HER TALKING TO GUYS... HE LOOKS A BIT MISERABLE!

Knowing Suzy was looking after someone who was ill only made her seem more perfect in my eyes...

I did feel a fool when it got round to the swimming bit though...

GUESS WHO?

YOU'LL NEVER LEARN TO SWIM IF YOU STAY THERE!

After about ten minutes, I think she gave up!

CHRIS, I THINK THERE'S ONLY ONE WAY YOU'RE GOING TO LEARN TO SWIM!

HOW ABOUT — THE ONLY PERSON I KNOW HERE?

BUT — IT'S FREEZING! JUST GIVE ME A FEW MORE MINUTES...

YEAH? WHAT'S THAT?

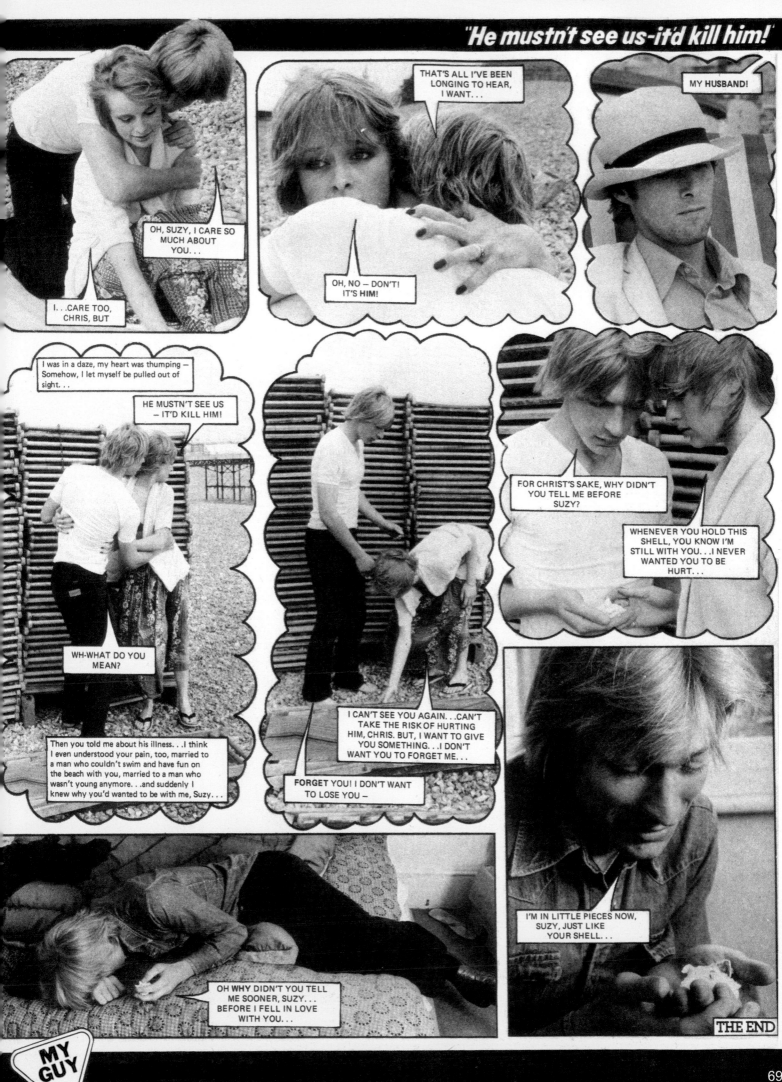

I DREAD ANSWERING THE PHONE

I keep getting obscene phone calls.

When I answer, a man's voice says horrible things to me then he just laughs and puts the phone down.

I have no idea who this can be, but the calls really scare me.

Now I daren't go out at night in case he's watching me.

I haven't spoken to my parents about this as I'm too scared.

Please help me as I'm very worried and frightened.

L. H., West Yorkshire.

I sympathise, obscene phone calls are very frightening and upsetting.

But doing nothing is only going to make you feel worse.

So first, please confide in your parents. It'll make you feel better just to tell them and they can do something practical to help.

For a start, they can answer the phone when it rings. If you never pick it up, the man may give up.

Your parents should inform the Post Office of what is happening. They may solve the problem by giving you a new phone number which is ex-directory.

This may be someone you know playing a silly joke. But what matters is the effect it's having on you, joke or not. Don't suffer in silence any more.

And if you do get caught again, refuse to say anything, just hang up.

Statistics seem to show that the people who make this type of call rarely do anything else, but you can't be too sure, so tell your parents today.

IT'S ALL LIES

After my first date with this guy, he took me home to his house.

His parents were out and he started to try it on.

I stopped him and went home.

But now he's telling everyone we had sexual intercourse.

I'm very embarrassed, so what can I do?

Janice, Glasgow.

Ignore him if you can, Janice. That's all he's worth.

If you're asked about the rumour, tell the truth. Say he's lying, then say no more.

The more you talk about it, the longer the rumour will last.

This boy is immature and anybody who knows him, probably won't believe him anyway.

HE'S A STICK-IN-THE-MUD

When my family go to a dance, they always ask me and my boyfriend to go with them.

But he never wants to go. He'd sooner watch the television!

Even if he does come, he never dances with anyone.

How can I make him see the enjoyment of going dancing and mixing with other people for a change?

Jan, Cannock.

You could start by being a little more understanding.

My guess is that your guy is shy. He probably goes through agonies on social occasions.

Then again you could look at the fact that it is YOUR family.

Sounds as if you could be lumping him in with the rest of them.

And if they're a lively bunch he probably sticks out like a sore thumb and hates being urged to join in all the time.

Some people just don't enjoy dancing, or crowds, and your guy could be one of them.

Either do what he wants some of the time, in the hope that he'll respond by joining your family fun occasionally, or face the fact that you don't have much in common . . .

WHEN HE CALLS I COME RUNNING

I have known my boyfriend for two years.

But he is always chucking me, then taking me back.

It's happened again. I'm really unhappy, as I love him.

But I know that if he asks,

IT'S NOTHING TO WORRY ABOUT...

It's a bit of a drag when all your mates are going steady, and you're not. But it's better than getting in too deep, too soon . . .

What does it mean when you go out with lots of boys but none of them ask you to go steady?
It doesn't mean there's something wrong with you. It's probably just that you haven't met a guy who wants to settle down yet.

And it could be because you haven't met a boy you want to go steady with yet. Boys sense this and don't ask!

Suppose you really want a steady, but can't find one?
Everyone wants a partner, eventually, but sometimes it takes a long, long time to find the right one for you.

Meanwhile, guard against wanting to go steady for the sake of it.

What do you do when all your

NOT HAVING A STEADY

friends have steadies?
Try not to feel jealous, for a start. Could be that most of them will find things don't work out anyway.

Never hang around your friends waiting for them to break up with their guys.

Go places where you'll meet other people.

True friends will find time for you *and* their guys.

What if you don't want to go steady?
Then make sure it's common knowledge.

People can be funny — and you don't want them saying you're a two-timer.

Let every boy you go out with know, gently, that you're not ready to settle for one person.

And then make sure you don't behave with any of them as if they WERE your steady . . .

Can you put guys off by wanting to go steady?
Yes, and guys can do the same to girls. If you give the impression you want to own him, then he's sure to run a mile.

Going steady comes naturally after you've got to know each other and decided that it's going to be just for you two for a while.

GOT PROBLEMS...

Don't bottle them up. If something's getting you down, drop me a line and I'll try to help. My name is Chris, and the address is: My Guy, 21st Floor, King's Reach Tower, Stamford Street, London SE1 9LS.

RAT OF THE WEEK!

This week's Rat had her plan all mapped out...

"*When a girl at school asked me and my mate to her party, I was quite excited, because I knew a guy I fancied would be there.*

I asked how to get to her house, but my mate said it was all right, she knew.

The day before, this mate told me she'd be late getting to the party.

Then she drew me a map of how to get there – the girl lived in the town next to ours and I didn't know it very well.

But that map was a load of rubbish. My 'mate' had jumbled up the roads so that I'd get lost. And I did.

When I finally arrived at the party she was there already – chatting up the guy I fancied!"

If you know a real Rat, drop me a line, marking the envelope 'Rat of the Week'.

I'll go back with him.
I can't talk to him about it.
Sandra, Sussex.
If you can't talk to him, he makes you unhappy, and he's always playing this dirty trick, why do you love him?

You may think that's a daft question, but think about it.

Love is sharing and caring. There doesn't seem to be much of that in your relationship.

Love makes you happy — so please stop making yourself sad, which is what you're doing.

Tell this guy you've had enough. If he can't make up his mind for himself, you'll do it for him — and find someone who thinks you're worth something and not just a toy to be played with when he feels like it.

SHE DRIVES ME TO WITCHCRAFT!
My friend is very common and enjoys being a vandal.

She bullies me and last week I didn't get invited to another friend's party because this girl didn't want me to go.

She gets the other girls to gang up on me, even though I'm kind and helpful to her.

I've even tried black magic on her.

Please help me.
10 cc fan, Islington.
I would usually advise anyone to be kind and helpful as a way to win over an enemy.

But this time I think you'd do better to keep your kindness for others.

For a start, forget the black magic — black thoughts make normally nice people nasty.

And you don't want to be as unpleasant as she is, do you?

Then stop thinking of this girl and her cronies as friends. Friends are friendly — these girls are not.

Try to find a different bunch to go around with. There are plenty of young people to choose from where you live.

Be polite to this girl if you see her, but steer clear if you can.

MUM SAYS HE'S TOO OLD
I've fallen for a guy who works with my mum.

I go to her work quite a lot and I'm sure he likes me.

But she says he's too old for me. He's 21 and I'm 15.
What do you think?
Punk fan, Birmingham.
I think that what your mum thinks is more important than what I think, if you see what I mean.

She knows the lad in question, and she knows you.

It's not always a matter of your actual age, but more how grown up you are — and everyone grows up at a different rate.

I doubt that your mum is objecting simply because of the age difference. It's more likely that she just doesn't think you're suited.

So my advice is listen to your mum.

If this lad asks you out, talk it over with her.

I'M SO MIXED UP
My sister packed a boy up because she says, she doesn't like him.

Now he wants to go out with me. My dad says I shouldn't go out with my sister's ex-boyfriends.

My mum says none of the boys round here, including him, are good enough for me and my sister.

My sister says I'd be daft not to go out with him as I like him a lot. Help!
What shall I say to him?
Faye, Brighton.
Well, they've all got a point.

But what do you think? You're the one he really matters to.

Unless this boy's very special, I shouldn't think he's worth all the family hassle that's going on. And I'm sure there are lads around who would meet with eveyone's approval ... Just have a look around.

GUYS – I'LL HELP YOU TOO!

TWO GIRL TROUBLE
I have been dating two girls, But neither romance seems to be going very well.

Both of them argue a lot with me. I think it's because I'm seeing them both.

I don't want to break anyone's heart.

So, some advice please.
Eddie, Dunfermline.
Sounds as if both girls want to be your steady. As you're not ready to settle down, and are making no secret of the fact that there's more than one girl in your life, that's what they'll have to accept.

But as both of them don't seem able to treat the relationship as casual, they're getting hurt.

So it would be kinder to finish with them both, and go out with girls who don't want to get serious with you.

JUST GOOD FRIENDS
A girl called Jane and I have to help the caretaker at school.

I really like Jane, but just as a friend. And that's how she feels.

But the caretaker is always hinting that Jane and I will fall in love. It upsets us.
Robert, Staffordshire.

He sounds like a silly man. But that's all. He's just having a joke with you.

Either ignore him, or joke back. Try telling him, laughingly, that he's very clever, how did he guess you were planning to run away to Gretna Green, get married and raise a family of eight! If you and Jane go on about it, he'll probably get tired of the subject.

I CAN'T KISS
I am 12 and there are a lot of girls I would like to date.

Trouble is I don't know how to kiss properly.
Can you help?
Tony, Crieff.
There are far more important things to be thinking about, Tony.

Like how to put a girl at her ease. How to make her feel special. Kissing comes naturally after you've found someone you care for and who cares for you as well.

There's no 'proper' way to do it. The mistake is in kissing too soon.

So relax. Most girls of your age don't want to be kissed straight away anyway.

MARKED FOR LIFE?
I have a cross tatooed on my arm.

It's been there for two years but now I desperately want to get rid of it.

Someone told me to cut it and put ink remover in it.
Is this a good idea?
P. B., Buxton.
No, it's a terrible idea. In fact, it could make you very, very ill.

Go to see your doctor immediately. He'll know what to do.

And please, please don't do anything yourself. It could be very dangerous.

Perfect Partners Or JUST GOOD FRIENDS?

YOURS

1. If a girl asked him to dance, would he:
(a) Accept immediately?
(b) Accept after getting the OK from you?
(c) Refuse?

2. It's a toss-up — between buying a vital new part for his car and your birthday present. Would he:
(a) Put his car first?
(b) Put you first?
(c) Compromise and take you out in the car?

3. To him, the thought of meeting your parents is:
(a) Not on the cards?
(b) A necessary evil?
(c) Nothing to worry about?

4. His way of paying you a compliment is:
(a) To tell you you look nice?
(b) Smile appreciatively?
(c) Keep quiet?

5. His favourite way of spending an evening is:
(a) Playing football?
(b) Watching T.V.?
(c) Going to the cinema?

6. Which of these is his favourite food:
(a) Fish and chips?
(b) Steak?
(c) Spaghetti Bolognaise?

7. What annoys him most:
(a) Cruelty to animals?
(b) Smoking?
(c) Football hooliganism?

8. Does he think the most important thing in the world is:
(a) Money?
(b) Love?
(c) Fame?

How much do you really know about your guy? And how much does he know about you? Do our special test and find out!

First, answer the questions (about him) in YOUR section (as best as you can!) and get him to answer the questions (about you) in HIS section!

Then, swap 'em over so that you're answering the questions in the HIS section and he's answering the YOURS section. Now check at the bottom of the page to find out just how suited you are!

HIS

9. Does seeing a film like 'Love Story' make her:
(a) Cry?
(b) Laugh?
(c) Sleepy?

10. Which of these would please her most:
(a) A candlelit dinner?
(b) A night out at the disco with your friends?
(c) A lazy day by the river?

11. What first attracted her to you:
(a) Your eyes?
(b) Your hands?
(c) Your smile?

12. Does she worry about her figure:
(a) Constantly?
(b) Occasionally?
(c) Never?

13. If it's late, she's lost her purse and she has to get home on her own, does she:
(a) Ring you up?
(b) Get a taxi and pay at the other end?
(c) Go to the police station?

14. She tries to get her own way by:
(a) Flattering you?
(b) Nagging you?
(c) Ordering you?

15. If a workman whistles at her in the street, does she:
(a) Ignore him?
(b) Give him a quick smile?
(c) Blush furiously?

16. What colour are her eyes:
(a) Brown?
(b) Blue?
(c) Green?

WE'LL TELL YOU!

Find out how you did by counting up the number of answers that you and he agree on. Now check your score!

12-16: *You two must know each other like the backs of your hands!*

You really appreciate each other. And, what's more important, thoroughly appreciate the best ways of making the other person happy.

And, as you understand each other so intimately, you must love every little thing about each other.

You're probably very well-suited and could easily be perfect partners for life.

The only danger lies in letting your whole relationship become stale and over-predictable. Keep the excitement going by giving each other a few surprises from time to time!

7-11: *You know each other pretty well, probably just well enough in fact, as you're still at the exciting stage of discovering each other's unknown qualities!*

There's still an element of mystery in the air that gives your relationship an extra spark. If you're happy with what you've learnt so far, you're probably both eager to find out more.

And, if that's the case, you could well end up as more than 'just good friends'!

But tread carefully, give yourselves time and don't expect too much from each other. Never take things for granted, just be thankful for what you've got.

2-6: *To be frank, you really don't know much about each other.*

The burning question is, do you care enough to want to be interested and learn more?

Perhaps you're both more concerned with yourselves and can't be bothered to take the time to learn about each other. But, if you want to make a success of your relationship, you've got to work at it.

For a happy, stable relationship, you, as two individuals, should try to think as one person more often.

So forget about yourselves and concentrate on each other. Consider his/her feelings more and a whole new world could open up.

Under 2: *Either you've just met or your relationship is a classic example of opposite personalities attracting one another!*

There doesn't seem to be anything that you do know about each other.

A good relationship isn't built solely on the grounds of having things in common. It's also a question of discovering what interests the other person has and being interested in them yourself — for their sake.

You've got to care enough about the other person to sense how they feel and react accordingly.

At the moment you're not even good friends — acquaintances is more like it.

Either get to know each other better, (go on, give it a try — it'll be lots of fun!) or look around for someone else to love!

TOO MUCH TOO YOUNG?

Des was young and in love and Tony had to do something about it!

Tony had just come home from a course he was doing in the north.

IT'LL BE GREAT SEEING DES AGAIN AFTER ALL THIS TIME! I DON'T SUPPOSE HE'S CHANGED AT ALL.

IT'LL BE JUST LIKE OLD TIMES ...GOING OUT EVERY NIGHT, CHASING GIRLS!

Tony didn't waste any time in ringing Des.

DES? HI, REMEMBER ME?

OH. ..HELLO, TONY. ER, HOW ARE YOU?

YOU DON'T SOUND TOO HAPPY. NOTHING WRONG IS THERE?

WELL, NOT EXACTLY NO, I ER. . .

But Tony managed to persuade Des, and they met at one of their old girl-hunting haunts.

DES! IT'S GREAT TO SEE YOU AGAIN, HOW'S TRICKS?

Des seemed to have something on his mind.

...MEET YOU FOR A DRINK?

WELL, THAT'S A BIT DIFFICULT, TONY, YOU SEE...

ER. ..HI, TONY.

LISTEN, I THOUGHT WE COULD GO ON TO A DISCO TONIGHT, YOU KNOW, TAKE A LOOK AT THE NEW TALENT? THE GIRLS AROUND HERE CERTAINLY HAVE IMPROVED SINCE I LEFT!

UM, LISTEN, TONY, THERE'S SOMETHING I OUGHT TO TELL YOU. . .

My Guy Likes... SUMMER...

Ok, so it might just be a memory away, but let's look forward, too... to a '79 Summer that'll be the Big One. If you

Bob and Andy chose these four outfits for us and even helped out at the photo sessions (wonder why?)...

THE FUN TIME!

choose outfits like these, and stock up on our My Guy Beach Kit, we guarantee you'll have a ball and a half!

THE KIT YOU CAN'T DO WITHOUT:

Beach bags have to be bigger than normal handbags just to carry all your gear this summer.

For a start, there's the essentials like tanning oil and make-up — but most important is that beach kit for getting the fellas!

Okay, there's a different way of getting to know him, depending on if he's yer intellectual type, or just plain hunky.

F'rinstance, the nicely skinny bloke with the glasses must be a bookworm so you carry a thick, hardback, volume of 'War and Peace' in your bag.

Then pretend to read it with great interest, having first of all made a huge noise about settling onto your towel in that scanty bikini.

If you own a pair of specs all the better cos when he approaches you for a chat, you casually tip the specs to the end of your nose and look over them at him. We guarantee his bookish heart'll melt.

Another 'must' for your kit bag is an inflatible beach ball. Now, they're meant to attract yer hunky, muscles and no brain type. When you see one approaching, casually get the ball from bag and proceed to blow... but make sure none of the air gets in to inflate the ball!

Then pretend to blow harder and harder. Mr Fixit'll come to your rescue and then, when he's finished with it, invite him to play ball with you.

If this fails, take up sunbathing!

OUT OF THE DARKNESS

Carol waited in darkness for help to arrive, but danger was moving in.

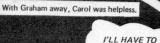

With Graham away, Carol was helpless.

I'LL HAVE TO RING FOR HELP.

NOW THERE MUST BE AN EMERGENCY SERVICE FOR ELECTRICITY, THERE MUST BE!

HELLO, IS THAT THE ELECTRICITY BOARD? YOU MUST COME RIGHT AWAY, I'M IN TERRIBLE TROUBLE!

I HOPE THEY CAN FIND THIS PLACE, I'M SURE I MUDDLED THOSE DIRECTIONS

DID WHAT?

KILLED A YOUNG GIRL THAT WAS STAYING HERE. NOBODY ROUND HERE WANTS TO LIVE IN THIS PLACE — NOT SINCE HE KILLED THAT GIRL

I DIDN'T KNOW HE'D ESCAPED THOUGH

OH MY GOD, I KNEW THERE WAS SOMETHING ABOUT THIS PLACE!

The telephone rang.

EXCUSE ME, I MUST ANSWER THAT

Carol hoped it would be Graham.

But she was wrong.

IT'S THE ELECTRICITY BOARD FOR YOU. I THINK THEY WANT TO KNOW HOW YOU'RE GETTING ON

As he passed her, Carol noticed something strange.

THAT'S FUNNY, I DIDN'T NOTICE THAT BEFORE, HE'S LIMPING VERY BADLY

And then —

WHY DID YOU PUT THE PHONE DOWN, THEY WANTED TO SPEAK TO YOU

THAT'S THE TROUBLE WITH THEM. THEY ALWAYS WANT TO SPEAK TO YOU — ALWAYS WANT TO KNOW WHEN YOU'VE FINISHED A JOB

The man from the Electricity Board, placed the receiver on the table.

There was something about him that unsettled her. She gazed down at his limping leg.

Outside slumped in the drive, lay the body of the Electricity Board man . . .

IF YOU DON'T MIND I'LL LEAVE IT OFF THE HOOK. DON'T WANT THEM PESTERING US AGAIN DO WE

WHAT'S HE DOING THAT FOR?

Carol began to feel uneasy.

AND THAT'S ANOTHER THING, HE'S GOT MUD ALL OVER HIS TROUSERS!

But there was something important, Carol didn't know.

But if he was there — who was inside with Carol?!

MY GUY

Turn to page 138

PART ONE

YOUR SUPERNATURAL GUIDE TO GETTING A GUY!

BE A LOVE-WITCH!

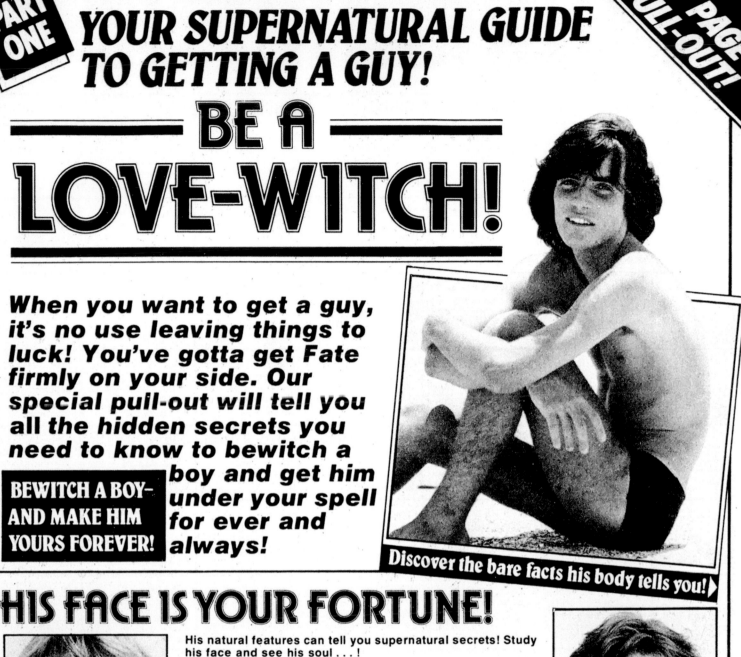

When you want to get a guy, it's no use leaving things to luck! You've gotta get Fate firmly on your side. Our special pull-out will tell you all *the hidden secrets you need to know* to bewitch a boy and get him under your spell for ever and always!

BEWITCH A BOY— AND MAKE HIM YOURS FOREVER!

Discover the bare facts his body tells you!▶

HIS FACE IS YOUR FORTUNE!

His natural features can tell you supernatural secrets! Study his face and see his soul . . . !

GOOD . . .
EYES wide apart — he's trusting and faithful.
Large, even *NOSE* — he has a strong character and is intelligent.
LAUGHTER lines — he's cheerful all the time and looks on the bright side!
MOUTH, nice and wide — he's generous and kind to others.
TEETH, even, white and shining — he's sensible and sensitive.
CHIN, firm and strong — he's the protective type you can lean on!

. . . NOT SO GOOD!
EYES, set close together — he could be mean and untrustworthy.
FROWN lines — watch out for his temper!
Twisted *NOSE* — could be aggressive.
Thin *LIPS* — not much sense of humour!
EYEBROWS, close — got a mind of his own, likes his own way!
HAIRLINE with strong widow's peak — he carries bad luck around – it could rub off on you!

HAVE YOU GOT HIS NUMBER?

There's magic in numbers, and it can work for you! All you need to know is your guy's birthdate, do some adding up — and his days of freedom are numbered!

For example, if his birthdate is 11th December, 1961, write it as 11.12.1961.

Add up the figures $1+1+1+2+1+9+6+1=22$. Then $2+2=4$. This is his Personality Number and tells you what he's *really* like!

What the numbers mean:
1. He's determined, proud and brave. Sticks to his guns.
2. A boy of extremes, very happy or very sad.
3. The perfect number! Luck is always with him — and with you!
4. He's sensible. A solid, kind and sympathetic fella, nice to have around.
5. A fast talker and fast doer too. He'll chat you up quick!
6. The peaceful type. Hates quarrels and never starts them.
7. A magic number! He's bright and well read. And he can probably read your mind!
8. He's loyal and will never leave you. A good judge of character — including yours! You wouldn't be able to hide anything from him!
9. Unpredictable and can't be tied down. He'll puzzle you — but never bore you!

YOU CAN HAVE POWER OVER BOYS!

83

SUPERNATURAL

YOU ↓ / HIM ▶	ARIES	TAURUS	GEMINI	CANCER	LEO	VIRGO
CAPRICORN	**Yes.** Your clear-headedness will make his ideas work. Together you could go far.	**Maybe.** You'll probably end up a little bored — but you could be happy.	**Yes.** You'll like the way he dashes around. But don't rely on him too much.	**No.** He'll not have enough push for your liking. And he'll be too soppy, too.	**Yes.** You could have the best time of your life with this one. But don't get hurt.	**Yes.** He'll admire your strength of character and tell you so.
AQUARIUS	**No.** You'll find him too sure of himself and not nearly considerate enough.	**No.** He'll never understand you. It's unlikely you'll have anything in common.	**Yes.** You're both air signs and that's good. He'll take you seriously.	**Yes.** You could do well together painting pictures or making music.	**Yes.** He'll be a bit on the tough side, but you'll like his basic honesty.	**No.** He'll not understand your love of dreaming. He's too practical for you.
PISCES	**Maybe.** You could be good friends. But he'll not be very sympathetic.	**Maybe.** He'll bring you down to earth and force you to commit yourself.	**Maybe.** But he might be a bit fickle for you. Don't misjudge him.	**Yes.** You're both water signs, but beware of getting swept away on a tide of emotion.	**No.** Don't be fooled into a romance, because it's unlikely to mean much to him.	**Yes.** He could be good for you. But you'll have to make him laugh sometimes.
ARIES	**Maybe.** Either very good or bad. Beware competition — neither of you will win.	**No.** You'll find yourself tied down when you want to get up and go.	**Yes.** You're both good with people. But you may have to play second fiddle at parties.	**Yes.** He'll always be there and he'll love the way you make him feel special.	**Yes.** A fiery time ahead. But let him take the lead or he'll leave in a puff of smoke.	**No.** After half an hour you'll be tearing your hair out at his tidy ways.
TAURUS	**Yes.** If you can persuade yourself to take a risk, he'll take it with you.	**Yes.** You could be happy together, but beware of getting bogged down in domesticity.	**No.** He'll make you feel a stick-in-the-mud when really you're just being sensible.	**No.** He'll bring out the worst in you — and you won't like him for it.	**Maybe.** He's a bit pushy, but he'll take you to some super restaurants.	**Yes.** He'll understand what makes you happy — and spend hours running treats.
GEMINI	**Yes.** You're both doers. But make him talk to you — it's your strong point.	**No.** He'll not be interested in going to parties or having a fun time.	**Yes.** If one of you lets the other get a word in edgeways. Don't be jealous of him.	**Yes.** He'll stick by you through all the messes you get yourself in.	**No.** He'll make you feel silly and laugh at the things that matter to you.	**No.** You'll find chatting this one up as much fun as banging your head.
CANCER	**Yes.** You bring out his best side. But be ready to be shocked out of a dream.	**Yes.** He'll appreciate your cooking and tell all his mates how great you are.	**Yes.** But you'll have to persuade him to stay around to realise it.	**Yes.** As long as you are both honest with each other and face up to reality.	**Maybe.** But he won't always want to sit at your side, so be prepared.	**Maybe.** But there's a danger that you could both be fooling.
LEO	**Yes.** As long as you let him decide what to do and where to go.	**No.** Because he'll think you're a show-off, and tell you so to your face.	**Yes.** He'll give as good as he gets and give you a good time.	**Maybe.** You'll have to be patient, though, and get to know him slowly.	**Yes.** You could end up very good friends, even if romance goes wrong in the end.	**No.** He'll think he's a weed. You're both wrong.
VIRGO	**No.** He's too untidy for you and his life's not at all organised enough.	**Yes.** He'll pay you compliments as long as you tell him he's wonderful, too.	**No.** You'll never be able to keep up with him — and quite probably won't want to.	**Yes.** He'll love the way you get him to talk about his childhood dreams.	**No.** He'll make fun of the things that matter to you, like being on time for dates.	**Yes.** Both of you like to know where you stand. But leave something to chance.
LIBRA	**Yes.** He'll love the way you give him freedom but lots of love as well.	**No.** He's too keen on material things for your liking. He won't understand you.	**Yes.** You two'll get on like a house on fire — but the flames could go out quickly.	**Yes.** Don't expect him to come on strong at first, 'cos he won't.	**Yes.** You'll let him get on with what he's doing and join in if he asks you to.	**Yes.** He'll be dependable but he'll let you get on with your life, too.
SCORPIO	**No.** You'll never be able to trust him. And he'll be wary of you, too.	**Yes.** You'll know where he is and what he's doing — as if by magic.	**No.** He'll be wriggling out of everything you plan and you'll feel let down.	**Yes.** He loves to feel that he's wanted — and you're the one to give lots of love.	**No.** He'll never let you feel sure of him, even if he's keen. A life of uncertainty.	**Yes.** He'll never let you down and he'll think you're very clever.
SAGITTARIUS	**Yes.** The best guy you could find. You'll have a great time and it could last.	**No.** He'll annoy you with his love of staying in and won't share your interests.	**Yes.** Rather an energetic romance this, but it could last a long time.	**No.** He'll make you feel tied and won't understand why you want some freedom.	**Yes.** That's if you'll both calm down enough to realise that you're in love.	**No.** He'll be too fussy for you and you'll be so lively he'll not have time to breathe.

LOVE CHART

Find out his star sign and you don't have to guess if you'll get on! Our Love Chart will tell you!

LIBRA	SCORPIO	SAGITTARIUS	CAPRICORN	AQUARIUS	PISCES	◄ HIM ／ YOU ▼
Yes. You'll love the way he's always fair and kind to your friends.	**Yes.** But don't let him boss you around or you'll feel fed up pretty soon.	**Yes.** Encourage him to put his ideas into practice and he'll love you for it.	**Yes.** You're both after the same things in life — success and popularity.	**No.** He's too much of a dreamer for you. You'll lose patience quickly.	**No.** You'll think he's wishy-washy and he'll think you're far too definite.	CAPRICORN
Yes. You could fall in love across a crowded room! And you'll be good friends, too.	**Maybe.** But open your eyes or you'll miss the subtle signs he's sending you.	**Yes.** As long as you're prepared to be a bit more practical.	**Maybe.** He could be good for you — make you feel important.	**Yes.** That is if one of you notices that the other's around soon enough.	**Yes.** He'll give you plenty to think about and you'll enjoy talking to him.	AQUARIUS
Yes. But don't try to tie him down straight away or he'll run.	**Yes.** He'll know he can trust you, so he'll relax and let the real him out.	**Yes.** But he won't be as understanding as you'd sometimes like.	**No.** You'll want to find the real him — and he won't let you.	**Yes.** You'll probably fight, but it'll be great fun making up.	**Yes.** But beware of both pretending to be something you neither are.	PISCES
Yes. He'll think all your loony ideas are great and you'll love his sincerity.	**No.** He'll be so possessive and jealous that you'll feel like you're in jail.	**Yes.** You two make an ideal couple — popular, good fun and very lively.	**Yes.** If you get on right from the start you'll probably stick together.	**Yes.** As long as you realise that you're not always the most important thing around.	**No.** You'll be unsympathetic when he feels like wallowing in a bit of self-pity.	ARIES
No. You'll find him much too airy-fairy. Not man enough to take you on.	**Maybe.** But don't expect him to be very passionate at first.	**Maybe.** He'll try to get you away from that fireside and out into the fresh air.	**Yes.** He'll know why you dislike too much chat and not enough do.	**Maybe.** But only if you both make a lot of effort to understand each other.	**No.** He's not enough of a leader and you won't enjoy pushing him around.	TAURUS
Yes. Definitely. You'll both spend your time on Cloud Nine — very romantic.	**Maybe.** But be careful of hurting him. If you do he'll get his revenge.	**Yes.** He's energetic enough not to make you feel stuck in a rut.	**No.** He's more likely to tell you to shut up than think your chatter interesting.	**Yes.** He's a good listener. And there's nothing you like better than chattering.	**Yes.** He'll think you're a real laugh. But let him compliment you if he wants.	GEMINI
Yes. He'll think you're sweet and you'll find him very understanding.	**Yes.** But you'll have to conquer your shyness to bring him out of his shell.	**Maybe.** He loves someone to come home to. But don't make him too sure of you.	**Maybe.** But you may not be able to keep tabs on him as much as you'd like.	**Yes.** He'll be faithful, but he might take you for granted if you let him.	**Yes.** You two could have a lovely romantic time. True love at its best.	CANCER
Yes. As long as you take him seriously. He's nobody's fool.	**No.** He's too secretive for you. And he's unlikely to open up for you, either.	**Yes.** But you could end up trying to outdo each other, friendly rivals, not lovers.	**Yes.** He'll like the way you get things done. But don't be bossy.	**No.** You'll be infuriated by him and he'll think you're trying to organise his life.	**Maybe.** But unlikely, as he'll never have the courage to ask you in the first place.	LEO
Maybe. He'll do some straight talking but you may not be too sure of him.	**Yes.** You'll make him feel loved, which is just what he wants.	**Yes.** But you'll have to learn to share him with his many friends.	**Yes.** He thinks you're sensible and you think he's pretty clever.	**No.** He'll never be sure of how he feels — even about you.	**Yes.** He'll tell you how much he depends on you — and you never let him down.	VIRGO
Yes. You'll both be glad you found each other — and tell each other so.	**Maybe.** You'll have to keep telling him he's the only one if you want to keep him.	**Yes.** He'll keep you guessing, but then that's the way you like it.	**No.** He'll always be trying to find out exactly what you mean — do you know?	**Yes.** He'll love the way you put his ideas into practice.	**Yes.** He'll make you feel important and he'll know what you mean instinctively.	LIBRA
Yes. This could be a whirlwind romance, don't let all common sense blow away.	**Yes.** And No. If you can learn to trust each other it'll be fine. If not — agony.	**No.** He's much too much of a roamer. You'll never know where he is or who he's with.	**Yes.** Dependable and says what he means. You'll appreciate his honesty.	**Yes.** He might keep you guessing, but he'll never laugh at you.	**Yes.** You're both good at finding unusual things to do. Now you can do them together.	SCORPIO
Yes. He'll be your biggest fan and is very likely to love the way you dress.	**Maybe.** He might be a bit of a wet blanket, though, so look out.	**Yes.** But try to find some time for romancing. You're both a bit lively.	**Yes.** He'll give you a run for your money — but you'll catch him in the end.	**Yes.** But you'll have to calm down a bit to realise he fancies you.	**No.** He'll tell you to slow down before you think you've even got started.	SAGITTARIUS

85

Revealed!

THE BARE TRUTH ABOUT HIS BODY!

A look at his bare body will reveal a lot about your guy! Try and catch him on the beach or get a photo of him in his trunks. Then study him carefully – and he won't be able to hide a thing!

HAIR Straight — he's straightforward. Curly — he's emotional and excitable.

NECK Short — he's stubborn. Extra long — he's a bit of a dreamer. Hairy — he's secretive!

CHEST A lot of hair — he's a he-man and a boaster! No hair — he's shy and unsure of himself.

BACK Hairy — don't trust him!

TUMMY Hairy — he likes a good time, with anyone!

NAVEL Large — he's a Mummy's boy, tied to her apron strings. Small — he won't be tied down. Round — he's a fun-lover, good for a laugh! Crooked — he hates making decisions.

ARMS Long — he's competitive and hates losing. Short — a shy type who prefers a book to a disco.

LEGS Thin — don't be pushy, you'll scare him off. Well-rounded — a bit of a lad with the girls.

KNEES Knobbly knees means he can take a joke and will laugh at himself.

MOLES

The bigger they are, the more it's true!

On the shoulder — he has problems. On the left, with his family. On the right, at work.

On the arm — he's content.

On the chest — he's ambitious and will go far.

On the back — he needs reassurance.

On the tummy — he's got a temper.

On the thigh — he's passionate and sexy.

On the calf — he's soppy.

BOYS WILL BE POWERLESS TO RESIST YOU!

HOW DOES HE SHAPE UP?

A guy's body shape reveals a lot about him. There are three basic shapes. Make sure you get the right one!

The tall, skinny and athletic type is likely to be a healthy out-door guy. He makes a good friend and a keen lover!

Tall and going to fat he's a dreamer. Artistic, but fond of the good things in life, like food and drink. He's hard to tie down, so play it cool!

Short and stocky and he's cocky too! He loves giving his opinion and having rows! Just to convince you he's right. He's stubborn with it!

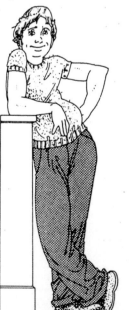

HOW HE DROPS 'EM

...AND WHAT IT MEANS!

If you can get him to tell you, or better still if you can watch, how he undresses, (maybe on the beach!) he'll reveal a lot more than his bare bod!

SOCKS: If he takes 'em off first, he's a sensitive type. Last, and he's the opposite, not much interested in the finer things in life.

SHIRT: If he unbuttons it and and then takes it off, he's much too fussy. If he pulls it over his head, he's impetuous, ready for anything!

TROUSERS: Watch out if he gets his jeans inside out when undressing. He's a mess and doesn't know whether he's coming or going! If he pulls 'em off from the bottom, he tends to be shy.

FOLDING CLOTHES: If he carefully folds each item, and lays it neatly in a pile, he's very fussy and hard to please. If he throws 'em anywhere, he's an open abandoned type. But not much fun to clear up after!

SHOES: If he puts 'em neatly together, he's a worrier.

If they're together but left where right should be, it means relationships confuse him. If one points one way, and one the other way, he's the moody type!

DON'T MISS PART 2!

You'll discover —

WHAT HIS DOODLES DO FOR YOU! YOUR FATE IN HIS HAND! WHITE MAGIC WAYS TO KEEP HIM SPELLBOUND! HIS BODY'S MOODS AND WHAT THEY MEAN! PLUS! SECRET LOVE-SIGNS HE CAN'T HIDE!

IT'S ALL HAPPENING NEXT WEEK!

What young girls should know about Tampax tampons

How do you start?

Everything you need to know will be found in the packet. An easy-to-follow instruction leaflet provides step-by-step illustrations that explain how Tampax tampons are used, and answers questions young girls frequently ask about menstruation.

Why should you trust Tampax tampons?

Tampax tampons come in two absorbency sizes for different needs. Regular and Super, in packets of 10 and the economy 40's. Since Tampax tampons give you invisible internal protection, no one will ever know you're wearing them. There are no bulges as you have with thick maxi-pads. And you've no need to worry about staining as you do with a mini-pad.

Look at the container-applicator. Its slender shape and smooth, pre-lubricated surface makes insertion easy, even for beginners. It guides the tampon into the correct position neatly, quickly and hygienically — your fingers need never touch the tampon.

What about disposal?

Like the Tampax tampon, the container-applicator is flushable and biodegradable and so does not contribute to the pollution of the environment. It comes apart in water and is as easy to dispose of as a few sheets of facial tissue.

Now, remove the tampon from its applicator. Feel how soft and flexible it is. Notice the way the withdrawal cord is chain stitched the entire length of the tampon. It can't pull off. Upon removal, the Tampax tampon slims itself so that it's as easy and comfortable to withdraw as it is to insert.

How old should you be to use tampons?

If your periods have started, you're old enough. Tampax tampons slip easily into the same opening that channels the menstrual flow from your body. So there's nothing for you to be concerned about. Try Tampax tampons — you'll find many reasons to trust them.

TAMPAX
tampons

The internal protection more women trust

MADE ONLY BY TAMPAX LIMITED, HAVANT, HAMPSHIRE

SISTER BLACKMAIL!

Trying to take love away from her sister was Deidre's first mistake–and her last!

I'd been waiting and hoping for Gary to come round all day, but now he was the last person I wanted to see . .

HOW CAN I DO IT? HOW CAN I MAKE HIM GO WITH DEIDRE WHEN I LOVE HIM SO MUCH? BUT I'VE GOT TO. . . IF HIS MUM SEES THOSE PHOTOS IT'LL KILL HER!

When the doorbell rang, I was out of the room like a shot!

BETTER HURRY, DEAR . . . WE DON'T WANT TO KEEP MY BOYFRIEND WAITING, DO WE?

GOD, I WISH SHE WAS DEAD!

I felt tears of rage burn my eyes, but I blinked them back and rushed downstairs . . .

HI . . . YOU OK?

I – I SUPPOSE SO. . .

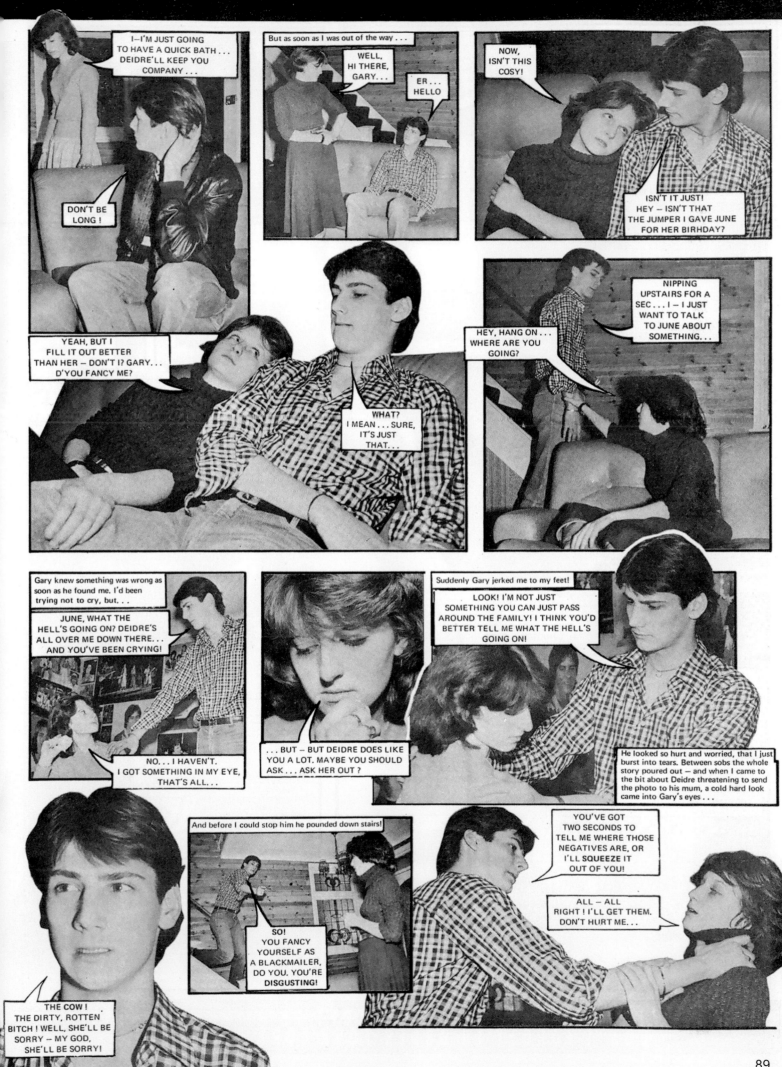

MARKED PERSONAL

I WOULD'VE KILLED TO KEEP HIM!

He was hers – but Julia knew Mike just couldn't be trusted . . .

THE FIRST night I saw Mike, I fell in love with him. It was as simple as that. He was standing on one side of a room at a party. I came through the door from the hall — and bang! We sort of looked at each other and smiled, then with all those strangers in between us, we started pushing past so we could get to each other.

It was the most incredible thing that has ever happened to me, and soon we were standing side by side, like we'd been doing that always.

"Hi!" he said, and his mouth gave a funny little upwards twist when he smiled. "Can I get you a drink or something?"

"Not really," I stuttered like an idiot. "I'm not thirsty."

"Oh." He frowned at me. "Fancy a dance then?"

There was a really slow, smoochy album playing, and as soon as Mike took me in his arms I just *knew* I never wanted him to let me go again.

In fact, we stayed together for the rest of the evening, he saw me home, 'n when we were stopped outside my gate eventually said, ever so shyly, "D'you want to go to the cinema, tomorrow? There's supposed to be quite a good movie on down at the Regal. I'll pick you up, if you like."

When I nodded, he leaned across, kissed me and said, "See you tomorrow."

I could hardly sleep for excitement that night. I kept going over and over everything that had happened, picturing the way it'd all been but somehow I couldn't really believe that someone as fabulous as Mike — could really get involved with somebody plain 'n' boring like me.

Only he did. Soon we were seeing each other practically every night.

JEALOUSY

The trouble was, when we *weren't* together — I used to sit 'n wonder what he was doing, who he was seeing, who he was smiling at now. It was stupid, but I couldn't help it. I really loved him, and I couldn't bear the thought of him being with someone else.

If we wound up a date early for some reason, I'd go mad convincing myself that we were finished, that he was with another girl.

Sometimes, when he told me he had to work late, I'd flare up at him and ask him what he thought he was playing at. But he'd just give one of those gentle, turned-up smiles, put his arms round me and murmur, "Don't be silly, Julia. I'm not playing at anything. Trust me a bit more."

But my jealousy got worse 'n' worse, so

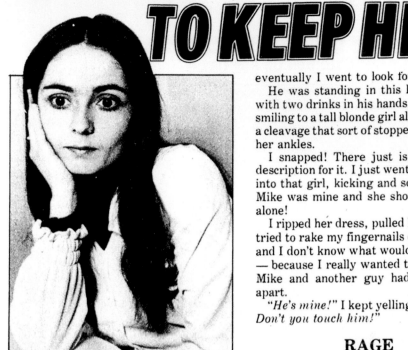

★ "I couldn't bear the thought of him being with someone else . . ."

that on nights when we weren't meeting I'd ring him, maybe four or five times, just to check that he actually *was* at home, or at work, or wherever.

It was like something had happened inside my head, and the more I tried not to think about Mike and other girls — the more it seemed to me that I couldn't *possibly* be the only person he was taking out.

I even used to go through his jacket and coat pockets when he was round at my place — just in case I found a letter, or an address, or even a girl's name. But there was never anything.

It got so bad that even when we *were* together I'd start asking him questions about his old girlfriends an' what they'd been like. Whether they'd all been older than me, or better-looking.

Now, looking back, I don't know how he stood it, but he was as patient as anything with me. He used to put his arms round me an' tell me I was the only one who mattered to him. But although he never snapped at me or anything, he never answered my questions, either — an' that made it all a lot worse, because I'd get certain all over again that there *was* someone else.

Then one night, after we'd been going around together for nearly two months, we got invited to this party. I didn't really want to go, but Mike was quite keen on the idea, and I started off thinking that maybe there was somebody there he'd said he'd meet. So although I was a bit quiet at the do, I stuck close to him, sort of hanging onto him like — an' the only time we ever really separated was when he went to the toilet.

I was watching for him to come back, and he seemed to take an awful long time, so

eventually I went to look for him.

He was standing in this kitchen place, with two drinks in his hands, chatting and smiling to a tall blonde girl all in black with a cleavage that sort of stopped round about her ankles.

I snapped! There just isn't any other description for it. I just went wild and tore into that girl, kicking and screaming that Mike was mine and she should leave him alone!

I ripped her dress, pulled her hair, even tried to rake my fingernails down her face and I don't know what would've happened — because I really wanted to kill her — if Mike and another guy hadn't pulled us apart.

"He's mine!" I kept yelling. "I love him! Don't you touch him!"

RAGE

The girl was screaming that she'd just been *talking* to him, but the same kind of blind rage that'd started me off in the first place was still churning through me — and I spat in her face.

I think it was Mike who slapped me, I'm not sure because I started to shake and tears poured down my cheeks. But I *know* it was Mike who said, "You're a fool, Julia. Come on. I'm taking you home."

He apologised to the girl I'd been fighting with, then he just grabbed me by the arm and walked me out of that party.

He took me right up to my own front gate, but instead of kissing me goodnight or anything, he stared at me — really coldly. "I don't think we'll be seeing each other again, do you?" he said eventually. "I can't live with your kind of jealousy, and God knows — I've tried."

Then he turned on his heel and headed off down the street.

I haven't heard from him since, and although I see him sometimes laughing or joking with some girl or other, he always turns away if he notices me.

I've given up crying about it now, because it *was* all my own stupid fault for not trusting him as much as I loved him.

And that's the trouble, you see. I still *do* love him. But after the way I behaved I'm never going to get a second chance to prove it. Am I?

PERSONAL

My Guy
Kings Reach Tower
Stamford Street
London
SE1 9LS

TV Fun TIMES

★★★★★★★★★★★★★★★★★★★★★★★★★★★★★★★★★★

THIS WEEK STARRING: Rolf On Any Day — Definitely Not O.K.!

The page that's got all the best (and worst) laughs on the box. And you don't even need a licence to read it — not yet anyway!

★★★★★★★★★★★★★★★★★★

TELLY TEASERS

It's another quiz, kids! And if you get all the answers correct — don't bother writing into us — we don't like bigheads. (Or big thighs either – Andy!)

1. We all know about one right Charlie and his angels — but what are the Beeb's heavenly bunch?

2. . . . And where do they work?

3. Who went to pieces after leaving Magpie?

4. Who is it that introduces Whodunnit?

5. . . . and what famous Doctor did he used to play?

6. Leonard Rossiter, seedy landlord in Rising Damp — what did he do before he took up acting?

7. At what age are you past it on 'Logan's Run'?

8. And where do you go to die?

ANSWERS AT BOTTOM OF PAGE

TURN ONS...TV TURN OFFS...TV TU

" . . . Biggest turn off I know is the Fonz. Yuk! His greasy hair and stupid voice make Saturday Unhappy Days for me" — **June, Slough.**

" . . . What's so funny about Crossroads? As far as I can see, all that's wrong with it is the acting, the actors, the idea, the script etc.," — **Noele Gordon Fan (!) Cheshunt.**

" . . . I love him, adore him, worship him. More Dennis Waterman please!" — **Sandie, Warwick.**

PAGE 4 COR!

Who do you fancy on the box? Write and tell us and we'll print his pic!

OLD NICK'S BACK!

GOOD to see Paul Nicholas back on our screens after so long!

Gorgeous Paul, who made his name in the hit musical Hair, has been making a hit with us ever since with singles like 'Grandma's Party' and 'Heaven On The Seventh Floor'.

He's recently returned from filming Sgt. Pepper in L.A. and assured us both his feet are now firmly on the ground — ready to get stuck in to his new TV show. Nice to have you back, Paul!

SHAME!

The spot where we offer consolation to those who live with the stars — and can NEVER switch 'em off!

TIE ROLF HARRIS DOWN SPORT (PLEASE!)!

THIS week we're saying stay down under to relatives of Rolf Harris.

They must be the only Aussie family who didn't give a relative a boomerang as a leaving present — in case he *did* come back.

Well, how would you like it if every time you tried to have a serious conversation with him, he got his didgeridoo out!

All the walls would be covered in his highly un-aboriginal drawings. And if you tried to stop him, he'd set his dingo dog on you!

The only highlight of your life would be when you got a throttle-hold on his stylophone!

Go on cobber — be a sport. Get back down under!

(Preferably three feet under – Andy!)

BACK IN A MINUTE!

The spot where we take a break for an ad!

BIG E. STRIKES AGAIN!

WHY have elephants got big ears?

'Cos Noddy wouldn't pay the ransom!

And it doesn't look like he's going to get the chance after Old Big Ears has finished with him.

The reason Big E's going to 'plaster' poor little Nod is 'cos he doesn't think much of his Vymura colour schemes!

Not surprised. Well, would you listen to a stupid dwarf dressed in *red, blue* AND *yellow*, with a jangling bell on his bonce?

TELLY TEASERS ANSWERS

1. Nurses — (They could rub my leg better any time — Andy)

2. St. Angela's.

3. Susan Stranks (teach her to leave lovely Mick Robertson). She tears up pieces of card-board in Paperplay now!

4. John Pertwee.

5. Doctor Who (pardon?).

6. He was a seedy insurance inspector.

7. 30 (Same age as Julie's bust measurement — Andy!)

8. Carousel.

COMING SOON:

Cheryl Ladd quits! Julie stars in 'Charlie's Chunky Thighs'!

92

Legend of the Lake

Did the Lady of the Lake exist-or did she only live in Richard's mind?

Stephanie had nothing to do.

IF YOU KNEW WHAT YOU WERE DOING, YOU WOULDN'T DO THAT.

DON'T TELL ME, I'M ANGERING THE SPIRITS OF THE LAKE. KING MORDRED OF THE UNDERWORLD WILL RISE AND SLAY ME BEFORE YOU CAN SAY EXCALIBUR. COME ON RICHARD, I'M ONLY HAVING FUN.

IT WON'T BE FOR MUCH LONGER, BELIEVE ME. I LOVE YOU TOO MUCH TO LET YOU GO OVER SOME BOOK, BUT I HAVE TO GET IT FINISHED. . .SOON.

THIS IS WHERE I'VE GOT MOST OF MY INFORMATION FROM. IT'S A GREAT BOOK, IT WAS WRITTEN BY THE FOURTH EARL HAVANT IN THE SEVENTEENTH CENTURY, HE'S THE GUY WHO OWNED HAVANT HALL, ABOVE THE LAKE. EVERY SIGHTING OF THE LADY HAS BEEN WHEN THE STAR CLUSTER 'AMALTHEA' APPEARS.

That night.

I CAN SEE YOU'RE NOT TAKING MY BOOK SERIOUSLY, YOU MAY THINK IT'S A LOAD OF RUBBISH, BUT I CERTAINLY BELIEVE THE LEGEND OF THE LAKE.

OF COURSE I TAKE YOUR BOOK SERIOUSLY. I'M JUST FED UP WITH DOING NOTHING, WHILE YOU DO ALL THAT RESEARCH.

SO WHAT?

RIGHT, THIS IS WHERE YOU DO YOUR ROMEO BIT AND TAKE ME FOR A ROMANTIC WALK ROUND THE LAKE. AND DON'T YOU DARE MENTION YOU KNOW WHO. . .OR ELSE!

The lake seemed tranquil that afternoon, nothing could disturb the peace and quiet, or Steph's love for Richard.

Next day.

I'M GOING TO SPEND MOST OF TODAY READING STEPH. SORRY, IT'S NOT MUCH FUN FOR YOU IS IT? ONCE I FINISH THE BOOK I PROMISE I'LL BE A BETTER BOYFRIEND.

IT'S ALL RIGHT. I THINK I'LL TAKE A TRIP UP TO HAVANT HALL AND TELL THE PRESENT EARL THAT YOU'RE PINCHING THE COPYRIGHT TO ONE OF HIS ANCESTOR'S BOOKS.

YOU CAN TRY, BUT I DON'T THINK YOU'LL HAVE MUCH LUCK. THE FOURTH EARL OF HAVANT WHO WROTE THE HISTORY, WAS THE LAST EARL OF HAVANT. HE DIED YOUNG WITHOUT AN HEIR. THE BOOK'S UNFINISHED. . .IT MAKES YOU THINK DOESN'T IT?

I'M DEFINITELY GOING OUT ONTO THE LAKE TO-MORROW. STEPH'S RIGHT, I CAN'T AFFORD TO MISS A CHANCE LIKE THIS. A SIGHTING OF THE LADY COULD MAKE ALL THE DIFFERENCE TO THE BOOK. IF I DON'T GO OUT, I'LL REGRET IT AND THERE CAN'T BE ANY HARM IN IT.

As Richard watched, the quiet waters parted and a figure rose from the lake.

Her face had a strange beauty, a strange peace.

Slowly and surely she moved towards Richard.

It was the lady he was searching for, the legend of the lake.

Richard could not move, hypnotised by the vision before him.

She reached out and touched him.

But Richard had been dreaming, it was Stephanie who woke him with her touch.

WHAT'S THE MATTER, RICHARD? YOU LOOK AS THOUGH YOU'VE JUST SEEN A GHOST.

More than ever, Richard was determined to get the evidence for his book!

WISH ME LUCK STEPH. I'M GOING TO ROW OUT INTO THE CENTRE, I'LL BE BACK HERE TOMORROW MORNING. BY THEN WE'LL KNOW IF THE LADY REALLY EXISTS!

But that night.

I'VE GOT TO HAND IT TO RICHARD, WHEN HE WORKS AT SOMETHING HE REALLY DOES WORK AT IT. YOU WOULDN'T CATCH ME SPENDING THE NIGHT IN AN OPEN BOAT — HEY, THIS LOOKS LIKE A PAGE FROM HIS OLD BOOK.

"AMALTHEA — THE DAY OF LEGENDS"

I WONDER IF RICHARD'S SEEN THIS, HE SAID THERE WERE BITS OF THE BOOK MISSING.

"THE LADY OF THE LAKE WALKS THIS DAY. BEWARE ALL WHO SEEK HER OUT, THE LAKE IS HERS AND HERS ONLY. HE WHO AWAITS THE LADY AWAITS HIS DEATH AT AMALTHEA."

AND RICHARD'S OUT IN THE LAKE. HE COULD NEVER HAVE SEEN THIS. HE TAKES EVERYTHING ABOUT THE LEGEND SO SERIOUSLY, HE WOULD NEVER HAVE GONE OUT IF HE SAW THIS! ALL I CAN HOPE IS IT'S NOT TRUE, I CAN'T HELP HIM NOW.

NOT A SIGN OF HER, DAWN WAS TWO HOURS AGO, IT'LL SOON BE TIME TO GO IN.

But Richard could not see the hands from the water!

POP

with Andy

COUGAR'S ITTY-BITTY KITTY WASN'T SO PRETTY!

Ever wondered how cool-cat Johnny Cougar got his name?

"Well, I've always loved cats," Johnny told me. "I once had a dozen of 'em. And a mate of mine was working at a zoo.

"He gave me this pretty little cat that had been born there.

"But it soon grew to enormous proportions and started eating everything in sight – cushions, sofas, that kinda thing!

"Soon I hardly had any furniture left!

"It was then that I realised that I hadn't got an ordinary moggy but a cougar!!!

"It got so big that when it sat on my lap I couldn't breathe!

"So I gave it back to the zoo. But I did decide Cougar would make a great stage name.

"Better than my real name, which is . . . er . . . well . . . (you'll never believe this!) Mellenchamp!"

Miaow!

COR! HOW CORNY CAN YOU GET?

Life can be hard for a struggling band on the road. Long van trips, greasy meals in cheap cafes.

And some bands can't even afford to eat in greasy cafes! Like Bethnal, in their early days frinstance!

"We were so broke we couldn't afford a proper meal," Nick Michaels confessed.

"We used to like doing gigs out in the country around harvest time.

"On the way home we'd stop the van by a field, and climb over the fence with our bass drum.

"Then we'd load it up with corn on the cob!

"Then we'd cook it as soon as we got home. I love corn on the cob – but I gotta admit I was getting pretty bored with it by the time we landed our record contract!"

Now the lads can afford to go into restaurants there's one thing they never order. Three guesses . . .

DOUBLE DOUBLES BRING CHILD TOIL AND TROUBLE!

One fateful night that oohsome twosome, Tim and Keith Atack of Child dated identical twin girls. Result — chaos!

"We thought it'd be a laugh so we went off to meet them, feeling dead keen. Until they turned up — 'cos they were with two other girls, who were also (wait for it) identical twins!

"And if that wasn't bad enough, all four girls were wearing identical clothes!

"In the end I went off with one set of twins, and Keith went off with the other.

"Cos neither of us could sort out one twin from another each of us had a disastrous evening, mixing their names up. Never again! We've had enough of double trouble!"

£25 FOR YOU!

DOES ONE OF THESE BOYS BELONG TO YO

NAUGHTY NIGHTSHIFT...

Mr. Gammack, Mr. Thomson and Mr. Williams aren't a load of stuffy bank managers — they're members of a band named Nightshift.

"We got the name from the fact that we were working nights at a recording studio," explained Mr. Gammack.

"We just worked on tapes for other people there. But sometimes, when the manager wasn't around, we'd play silly love songs we'd written ourselves.

"Well one night we were mucking about doing just that when the manager walked in and caught us.

"We thought we were all gonna get a rocket!

"But we got a big shock. He liked our sound and the song so much that he joined in with us. And afterwards he suggested we should make records ourselves."

MG MG MG

Is Henry Winkler mean or just plain sensible? The story goes that recently in a Hollywood store he was happily purchasing a pair of boots until told the price — £125!! "You're kidding," gasped the Fonz — and dashed out of the shop!!

MG MG MG

Eddie Kidd fans — join the club! Write to: Eddie Kidd Fan Club, P.O. Box 16, Leyton Buzzard, Beds.

MG MG MG

Does Andy Gibb need any help with his love life? Stupid question really — of course he doesn't but until recently a friendly ghost was giving the baby Bee Gee a helping hand!

Rumour is that Andy's houseboat was haunted and that any girl who came aboard felt immediately compelled to give the delighted Andy a great big kiss! Sadly, he's now sold the boat — but we bet he's still getting the same results!

MG MG MG

Warren Beatty sexy star of Heaven Can Wait is engaged — on the phone, that is! Seems Warren spends hours chatting his girlfriends up on the phone, sometimes talking to one girl on the line whilst he's kissing another on the sofa! Don't call us, Warren . . .

BEEN HERE BEFORE?

THUMBS DOWN FOR EDDIE?

Eddie Kidd was born on June 21st under the star sign of Gemini.

Gemini subjects are the superstars of the zodiac, blessed with wit, charm and the ability to make friends wherever they go.

Because they are so talented, others are often jealous of them — but their enemies had better watch out, Geminis have ways of getting their own back!

In love Gemini subjects are very good at talking about their feelings. They write the best love letters — even if they don't mean a word of them!

In a previous life Eddie may have been a chariot driver in Ancient Rome. He was very successful in races, until one day when he ran over the Emperor's foot. So he ended up as lion food! Can't see that happening this time round!

FREE AND EASY!

CHEAP LAUGHS WITH JILTED JOHN!

If Jilted John's record makes you giggle here's your chance to get some cheap laughs! Very cheap, in fact, absolutely free.

We're giving away 20 copies of the single.

All you have to do is write and tell us the name of the guy in the song who pinches John's bird Julie!

First 20 to get it right get a freebie!

The address is: My Guy, 21st Floor, King's Reach Tower, Stamford St, London SE1 9LS.

POP

'Cos if he does, this could be your lucky day! Yup, we've been out and about snapping fellas in secret and, if you recognise one of these faces, you could get £25 out of your guy!

How d'you get your hands on those five big blue ones? It's dead easy!

For starters, all you've got to do is study these pics *very* carefully. Is there a face there that you know and love? (Dads and passing passions don't count!)

If one of the boys we've caught on camera is your guy, he's well on his way to getting to grips with that loot!

Now tell your guy about his lucky break!

'Cos if his picture is above, all he's gotta do to get £25 richer is fill in the coupon on this page (clearly, in ballpoint) and send it, in a sealed envelope, together with a picture of himself (a photo-booth one will do)

I'M HER GUY! (And we claim the £25!)

My name is...

And I live at..

My girl's name is.....................................

And she lives at.......................................

....

MAIL IT TO MY GUY

MY GUY COMPLETE LOVE STORY

Lyn was bored and lonely now that Mark had gone.

WELL WHAT'S IT GOING TO BE TONIGHT, CROSSROADS OR NATIONWIDE? THAT'S JUST ABOUT ALL I'VE GOT TO LOOK FORWARD TO THESE DAYS.

Her days seemed so empty.

ALWAYS SOMETHING THERE TO REMIND ME

Mark had gone, and the only thing left of their love was threatened...

But it seemed that they had.

The radio was her only companion.

...AND AFTER THE BREAK WE'LL BE HEARING ABOUT THE DEVELOPERS WHO'VE BEEN GRANTED PLANNING PERMISSION FOR OAKTON MEADOWS...

W-WHAT?

The D.J's words filled her with horror.

THEY CAN'T BE SERIOUS. THE LAND BELONGS TO THE COUNCIL, SURELY THEY WOULDN'T SELL IT!

...SO NOW THAT THEY'VE BEEN GIVEN THE GO-AHEAD, WORK SHOULD START WITHIN THE NEXT COUPLE OF DAYS...

THEY — THEY CAN'T. I WON'T LET THEM!

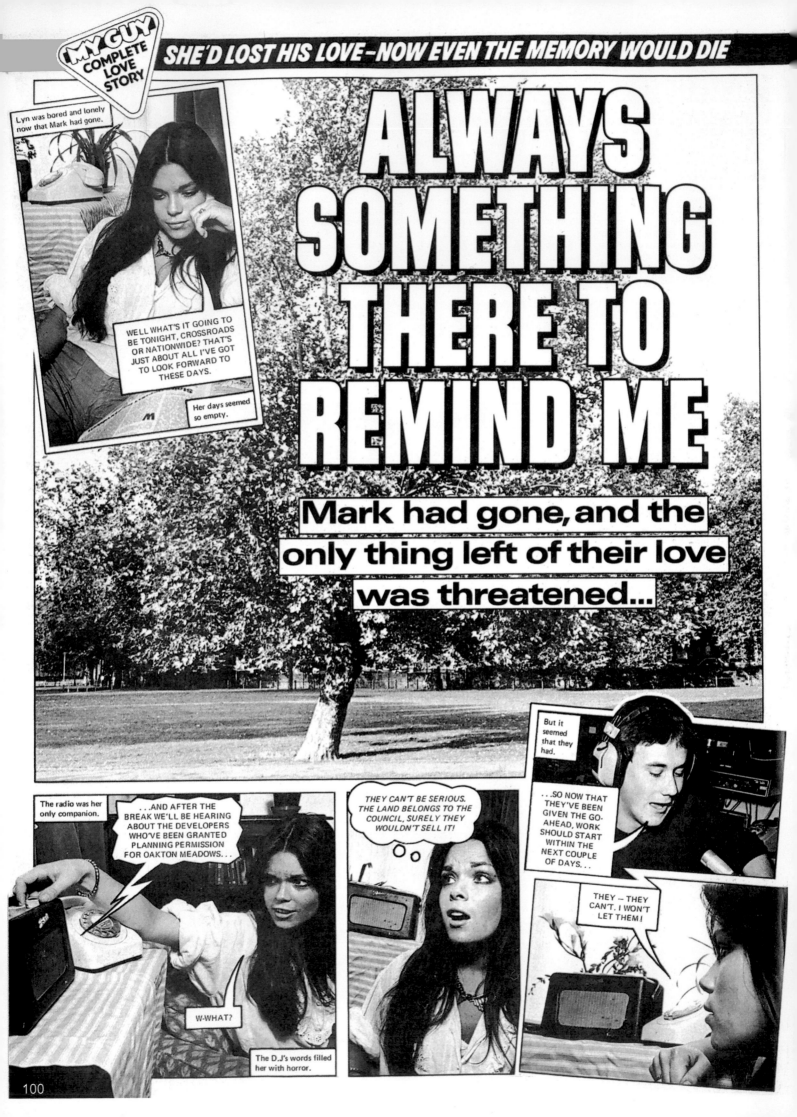

...AND IF THERE ARE ANY QUESTIONS THE LISTENING PUBLIC WOULD LIKE TO ASK THE LINES ARE NOW OPEN. THIS IS SIMON SELLARS AND I'LL BE BACK WITH YOU AFTER THE BREAK.

YOU BET THERE ARE SOME QUESTIONS!

So Lyn dialled the number.

HELLO, MY NAME'S LYN CAMERON AND I'M PHONING TO SAY THAT I THINK IT'S CRIMINAL TO DESTROY ONE OF OUR LOCAL BEAUTY SPOTS. FOR YEARS IT'S...

HI LYN, YES, THE COUNCIL HAVE ALREADY HAD A LITTLE OPPOSITION FROM PEOPLE WHO'D LIKE TO SEE THE SPOT PRESERVED, BUT AS I'VE ALREADY EXPLAINED THE NEED FOR NEW HOUSING IN THIS AREA IS SO GREAT...

I KNOW ALL THAT! IT'S JUST, WELL THE MEADOWS MEAN SOMETHING SPECIAL TO A LOT OF PEOPLE, THEY – THEY MEAN SOMETHING SPECIAL TO ME...

WELL THAT'S REALLY GREAT, LYN. WHY DONTCHA TELL US ABOUT IT!

I GREW UP IN THAT AREA AND ALL THE LOCAL CHILDREN USED TO PLAY THERE. BUT EVEN FROM THAT AGE I KNEW THE MEADOWS WOULD ALWAYS MEAN SOMETHING MORE TO ME...

Mark was the typical boy next door and as children we used to run wild through the Meadows, playing in the shade of the old oak tree...

We used to call it our special place and wait until all the other children had gone home, then come back and play till last light...

And as the years passed our friendship, like the tree, blossomed into something much more...

HAVE I TOLD YOU LATELY JUST HOW MUCH I LOVE YOU?

OH, NOT SINCE YESTERDAY!

And I thought that like the tree, our love would remain forever.

And the day when he carved our initials in the bark I could have cried with happiness.

OH, MARK, WHAT A LOVELY IDEA.

WELL IF I HAVE MY WAY YOU WON'T BE L.C FOR MUCH LONGER. HOW DOES MRS PARKER SOUND TO YOU?

I was just so much in love with him.

But after that things really changed. Once we were engaged it was almost as if he didn't have to try any longer.

THERE'S A DISCO ON AT THE BARRACUDA THIS WEEK. I QUITE FANCY GOING. WE DON'T SEEM TO HAVE DONE ANYTHING LIKE THAT FOR AGES.

WHAT'S WRONG WITH STAYING IN? IF WERE GOING TO GET MARRIED WE'LL NEED TO SAVE EVERY PENNY.

That was the trouble, Mark was just so dependable. Frankly, I was bored.

So when I met Gerry, I just didn't stop to think how much I had to lose.

THE BAND HERE ARE REALLY GREAT. I COME EVERY WEEK.

I CAN'T WAIT. I'VE BEEN REALLY LOOKING FORWARD TO THIS!

I really hated lying to Mark, I usually told him I was out with a girlfriend, but what else could I do..? Gerry was just so exciting.

A Girl's Best Friend...
IS HER BRA!

Undies are back! Back on your front, that is! So, forget all that stuff about burning your bra and slip into some of these — you'll be real hot stuff!

It ain't what you wear, it's the way that you wear it — and, to look really great, you've got to wear the right bra at the right time!

The flesh coloured satiny bra (top left) is perfect for wearing under slinky things so that they cling to your curves! From Littlewoods (£1.99).

Want a natural shape under a T-shirt? Try this no-bra, bra from Sunarama (top right). Don't wear this one under white though! Comes in loads of colours, costs £2.49 from most major department stores.

Palest grey and white bra (left) by Superotique (£5.50), from C & L Clayton, Bradford; Des Femmes, Boscombe. Wear it when you want to feel really feminine, to a party or on a special date. If you feel pretty, you'll look it! Or try this pale-blue boned bra (right) by Littlewoods (£1.99) for a bit of uplift so your plunge neck-line won't let you down!

Wear white under light, summery clothes — keeps you cool, won't show through. Pure white set by Sunarama (£2.49).

If you're wearing a strapless or halter-neck top don't sacrifice your shape! You can keep your bra on if you wear a strapless one like this one (right) from Marks & Spencer (£2.25).

TELLY-VISIONS!

THE KING OF COLA!

Cool it with Peter Blake. TV's answer to The Fonz in those Cola ads. Before doing his 'Sit on it' act Peter was a proper singer and he's had a few singles out. So maybe we'll hear much more of him in the future.

BOB-THE EYES HAVE IT...

Get some in! Which is exactly what actor Robert Lindsey has been doing. Besides being in that hit television series, Robert has other hobbies — models and the like. Free Sats will see Bob out on the nearest common with his super model radio controlled plane. He reckons it's not only an interesting pastime but the girls come up to chat and find out what he's up to. Smart lad!

...ONE FOR THE CHAPS' LOCKERS!

Recognise this angel? Right, none other than Cheryl Ladd, revealing a bit more than usual, 'specially for the Bob and Andy... (Back lads!)

SAINT OGILVY!

We reckon new Saint man, Ian Ogilvy is better to look at than Roger Moore. Agreed? So show us more, Ian!

KISS ME, HARDY!

Despite all our protests, the TV in Britain just aren't showing that super American show, The Hardy Boys. Which is a shame cos Shaun Cassidy and Parker Stevenson seem quite watchable...

MY GUY COMPLETE PHOTO STORY

THE GO-BETWEEN!

EVERYONE LIKES A BIT OF GOSSIP...UNLESS IT'S ABOUT THEM!

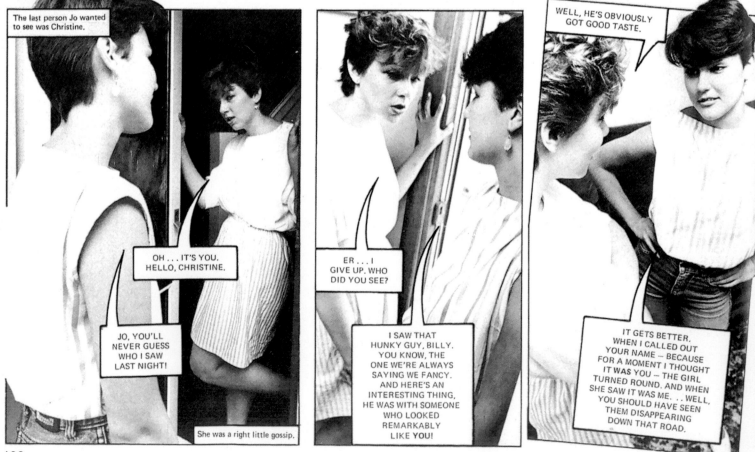

The last person Jo wanted to see was Christine.

OH . . . IT'S YOU. HELLO, CHRISTINE.

JO, YOU'LL NEVER GUESS WHO I SAW LAST NIGHT!

She was a right little gossip.

ER . . . I GIVE UP. WHO DID YOU SEE?

I SAW THAT HUNKY GUY, BILLY. YOU KNOW, THE ONE WE'RE ALWAYS SAYING WE FANCY. AND HERE'S AN INTERESTING THING, HE WAS WITH SOMEONE WHO LOOKED REMARKABLY LIKE YOU!

WELL, HE'S OBVIOUSLY GOT GOOD TASTE.

IT GETS BETTER. WHEN I CALLED OUT YOUR NAME — BECAUSE FOR A MOMENT I THOUGHT IT WAS YOU — THE GIRL TURNED ROUND. AND WHEN SHE SAW IT WAS ME. . . WELL, YOU SHOULD HAVE SEEN THEM DISAPPEARING DOWN THAT ROAD.

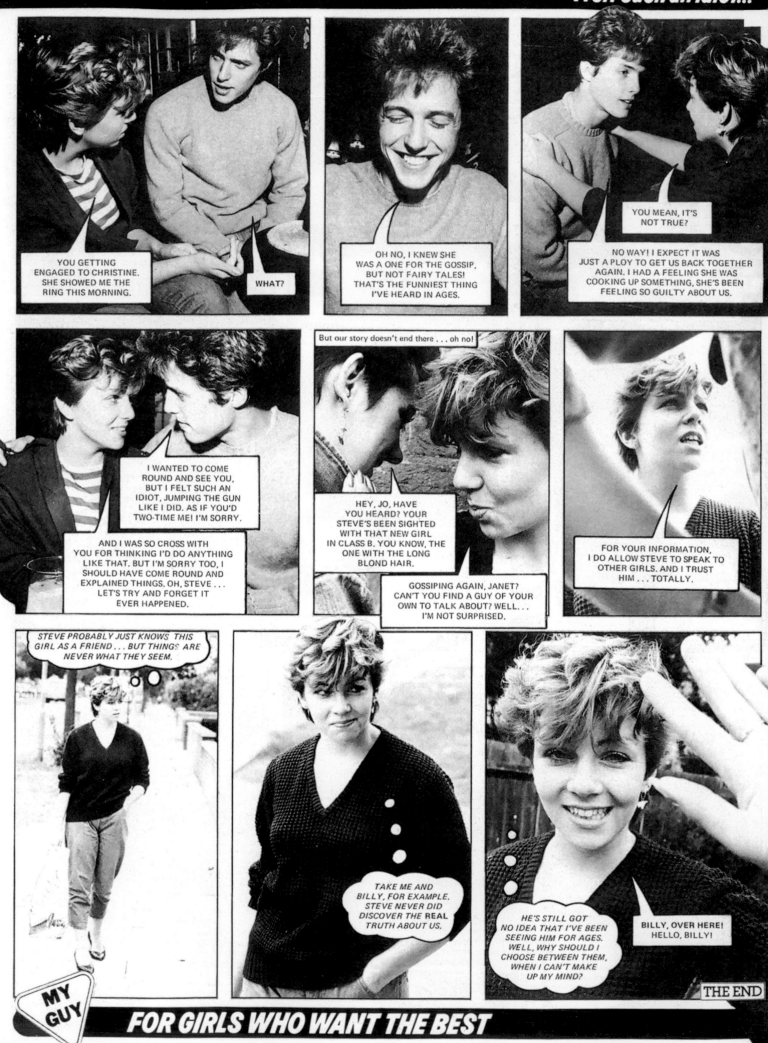

Blouses in Romantic Mood at C&A

There's a dreamy choice of blouses for you at C&A. Pleated front with lace trim. Or frill collar and tuck front. Or the blouson shape with scarf. Beautiful colours. Sizes 10-16. £5·95

C&A

such a surprising store

113

Attention! No giggling on parade! Belt-up, button-up — and get ready for a . . .

MILITARY COO!

TOP (Left): Shirt by Stirling Cooper £12.99 from Ronnie Stirling, New Bond St, London, W.1: Rackhams Birmingham. Medals £1.50 each, Sam Browne belt £6.50 both by Brighton Belle from Bentalls, Kingston. Oilskin pouch bag £3.99, leather tie from a selection by Baggage & General from branches of Snob & Van Allan. (Right): Shirt by Stirling Cooper £12.99. Gold medal £1.50 by Brighton Belle. Belt £2.70, silver stars 60p each by Oliver at Trimfit. BIG PIC (Left): Military coat comes with its own leather belt, sizes 8/14 from main branches of Wallis; side-cap just 80p from Laurence Corner. Angora gloves £1.50 from Boots. (Right): Cotton cord shirt £9.50 by Simon from Fenwicks, Brent Cross. 'Sarje' beret by Kangol £3.50 from major dept. stores. Red jacket by Monica Chong from Harvey Nicholls, W.1. Trousers by Stirling Cooper £14.99. Bow-tie £2.45 and top medal from B + G. Belt by Brighton Belle £6.50.

Many thanks to The National Army Museum, Royal Hospital Rd, London, S.W.3. for letting us take our pictures in their museum. They're open Monday-Saturday 10am-5.30pm and Sunday 2-5.30pm — why not take a visit, it'll give you masses of ideas for the current military trend!

GREAT GUNS — fashion's gone military mad! It's the order of the day and a right smart one at that! So, chest out . . . chin in and take to your uniforms quick. Yep, this is one fashion certainly worth saluting . . . just think of all those fellas advancing!!

BIG PIC (Left): The real thing (l) — red military tunic from Call To Arms, 79 Upper St., Islington, London, N.1. This one costs £18, but they do have a vast choice — write to them for more details. Black velvet trousers by Kobi £15.95 from Top Shop branches. Leather belt £2.50 from a vast selection at Badges & Equipment, 421 Strand, London, W.1. Hat 80p from Laurence Corner and leather bow-tie from selection by Baggage & General. **(Right):** Shirt £3.60, lanyard tied at shoulder 21p, red tie 40p all from Laurence Corner, 62/64 Hampstead Rd, London, N.W.1. Red velvets by Kobi £15.95. Belt by Call To Arms £3. Gloves £1.50 from Boots. 'Sarje' beret by kangol £3.50. **INSET (Left):** Jacket, shirt, and trousers all by Strawberry Studio in assorted colours, trousers £16.99, silky shirt £17.99 from their shop at 66 Old Compton Street, London, W.1. Diamante buckle belt £1.75, beads, and clips all by Baggage & General.

ARE YOU HANGING ON TO LOVE?

Do you know when things aren't going right and it's time to call it a day? Our quiz will tell you if you're hanging on too long . . .

1. Are you less jealous of other girls now than you were when you first met him? *Yes/No*

2. Do you think that he'll have to take you as he finds you, rather than dressing up in something special for him? *Yes/No*

3. Do you enjoy yourself when you go out without him? *Yes/No*

4. Do you ever find yourself wishing that you didn't have to see him tonight? *Yes/No*

5. Is there something about him — a habit or catch-phrase maybe — that irritates you like mad? *Yes/No*

6. Do you think that you'll break up someday, even if it does look like being a long time from now? *Yes/No*

7. Has he got any interests or hobbies which you hate, but put up with? *Yes/No*

8. Do you think you'd leave him if someone better looking with a nicer personality came along? *Yes/No*

9. Do you think he sometimes takes you for granted? *Yes/No*

10. Is he less thoughtful and polite than he was when you first met? *Yes/No*

11. Do you ever arrange things, like double dates or going to parties, without consulting him first? *Yes/No*

12. Do you avoid talking about the future with him? *Yes/No*

13. Do you sometimes wish you were free to go out and meet someone new? *Yes/No*

14. Is there anybody else you know who's more exciting than your fella? *Yes/No*

15. Does he listen more to what other girls say than to you? *Yes/No*

16. Is your social life with him less exciting than it used to be? *Yes/No*

17. Would you ever criticise him if you were talking about him to a mate? *Yes/No*

18. Does he ever stop you doing things you want to do? *Yes/No*

19. Do you think you could get a better looking boy if you wanted to? *Yes/No*

20. Do you find that he is predictable? *Yes/No*

21. Do you think your relationship is stuck in a routine? *Yes/No*

22. Is he less romantic than other boys? *Yes/No*

23. Would you talk over a problem with a mate, rather than with him? *Yes/No*

24. Do you think he's too possessive with you? *Yes/No*

25. Does he ever make fun of you in front of his mates? *Yes/No*

26. Are you ever nasty to him just for fun? *Yes/No*

27. Do you sometimes run out of things to say to each other so that there are long silences between you? *Yes/No*

28. Is he less generous with his money now, than when you first met? *Yes/No*

29. Do you prefer having lots of people around to being alone with him? *Yes/No*

30. D'you think that you were too young to go steady when you met him? *Yes/No*

31. Is there something about him that you'd like to change? *Yes/No*

32. Do you ever lie to him? *Yes/No*

33. Has he stopped buying you little presents? *Yes/No*

34. Do your mates' opinions of him matter to you? *Yes/No*

IS IT REALLY OVER?

If you answered mainly 'Yes':
Your relationship is pretty shaky, and it could be that you're hanging on to something that isn't worth it any more.

The trouble seems to be that you've got yourselves into a rut. You no longer find each other and the things that you do together, exciting.

You take one another for granted, and there's no reason why you shouldn't really, 'cos neither of you ever does anything to surprise the other and put a bit of spice into things.

You tend to remember the early days of first meeting and loving him. You look back on it as being much more romantic than things are now.

These days everything is flat and boring, and you are tempted to find someone else to get that old excitement back.

As things are, it's not much use hanging on any longer.

You should ask yourself if you really do love him, and if so, you should set about putting a bit more life into things. If you show him that *you* still care, maybe he'll respond and things will be great again.

But if he doesn't, then you might as well face facts and call it a day rather than let it drag on any longer.

But whatever you do, do it quick! Like now!

If you answered mainly 'No':
Your relationship is still on the 'up', 'cos you're still finding out about each other, and are liking what you find, too!

There are plenty of thrills and fluttering of the ol' hearts and life is still full of surprises for both of you.

So everything's rosy at the moment.

The only danger is that it might not be in six months or a year from now!

Y'see, at the moment you don't know one another that well. After a time any relationship becomes a bit more even, and the romantic whirl of first meeting levels out into something more routine and stable.

And that's when you have to put a bit more effort into things, to stop them going stale.

You'll find that after a few months you won't get butterflies anymore when you go out with him because you know him well enough not to be nervous and worried about what to say or what to expect.

So what you oughta do is tuck this quiz away somewhere safe, and try it again in a couple of months from now.

And if you find a few more of those 'Yeses' creeping in — you better get working on it quick!

MY GUY
COMPLETE
LOVE
STORY

'I'LL NEVER LET YOU GO'

Some girls will do anything to keep a boyfriend-anything!

I'd only taken Kim out a couple of times while my girl, Lynn, was away on a secretarial course. The trouble was, Kim had taken it much too seriously, and that made splitting with her very hard . . .

I'M SORRY, KIM, BUT IT'S OVER

BUT YOU DON'T REALLY WANT TO LEAVE ME, DO YOU ALEX ?

LOOK KIM, WE AGREED FROM THE START THAT IT COULD ONLY LAST TILL LYNN CAME BACK, AND SHE'S COMING HOME TODAY . . .

IT'S ALL RIGHT - I KNOW YOU DON'T WANT TO CHUCK ME, YOU JUST FEEL LOYAL TO THIS OTHER GIRL . . .

LISTEN, I LOVE LYNN – UNDERSTAND? AND I'M GOING TO BE LATE TO MEET HER. I'LL SEE YOU AROUND, OKAY ?

WAIT TILL I GET MY HANDS ON HIM, THE LYING TWO-TIMING...

HEY...THERE'S SOMEONE SPLASHING ABOUT IN THE BATHROOM - AND I BET I KNOW WHO IT IS!

Next thing I knew —

LYNN, WAIT! WHAT'S WRONG?

Without even looking at me, Lynn ran off down the street. I went back into the flat and found Kim getting dressed. I was furious, but Kim just stood there smiling at me. She just didn't seem to understand why I was so angry. I shouted at her, but she just kept repeating the same words; "I'll never let you go . . ."
Eventually I got really mad and threw her out, telling her that if she ever came back I'd make sure she'd regret it.
I phoned Lynn at home, but she hung up on me. I kept on trying though, and at last she agreed to meet me next day, to give me a chance to explain. By the evening I'd forgotten about Bev — all I could think about was Lynn and if she'd ever forgive me . . .

WHY DON'T YOU GO AND ASK THAT BITCH IN YOUR BATHROOM — BUT JUST DON'T COME NEAR ME AGAIN, YOU TWO-TIMING RAT!

I reckoned I was just feeling jumpy after yesterday, so I went to meet Lynn. If I'd only known what was about to happen . . .

THERE HE GOES — OFF TO MEET THAT OTHER COW, I'LL BET!

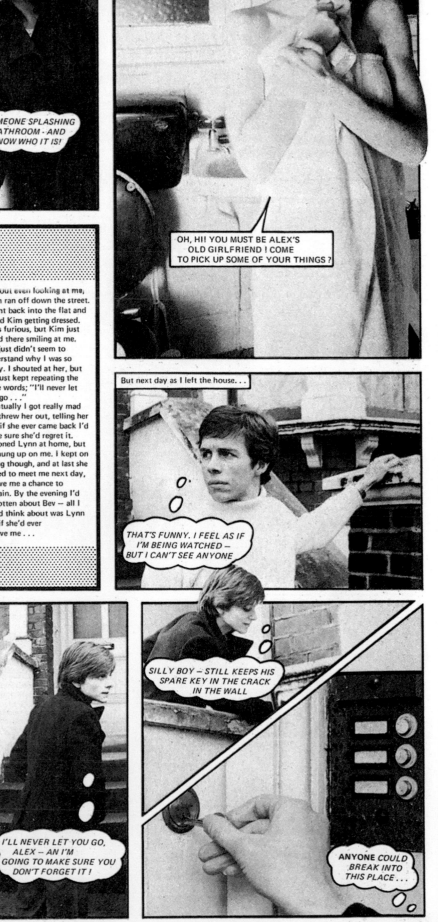

Lynn pulled open the door . . .

OH, HI! YOU MUST BE ALEX'S OLD GIRLFRIEND! COME TO PICK UP SOME OF YOUR THINGS?

But next day as I left the house. . .

THAT'S FUNNY. I FEEL AS IF I'M BEING WATCHED — BUT I CAN'T SEE ANYONE

I'LL NEVER LET YOU GO, ALEX — AN' I'M GOING TO MAKE SURE YOU DON'T FORGET IT!

SILLY BOY — STILL KEEPS HIS SPARE KEY IN THE CRACK IN THE WALL

ANYONE COULD BREAK INTO THIS PLACE . . .

I'M GOING TO CUT YOUR FACE INTO DOG MEAT!

OH NO YOU'RE NOT! COME ON, DROP IT!

OH MY GOD — LYNN!

I'd run round to the police station, and a detective had come straight back with me. It was just as well, 'cos Kim was completely out of her head . . .

LET ME GO. PLEASE. I'M NOT REALLY GOING TO HURT HER — I JUST WANT TO MAKE HER UGLY, THAT'S ALL

As he dragged her away, Kim spoke those words that sent a chill creeping down my spine . . .

I TOLD YOU, ALEX — YOU WON'T FORGET ME. I'LL NEVER LET YOU GO . . . NEVER . . .

BUT HAS SHE? HAS SHE REALLY GONE?

And in my worst dreams, on lonely nights, I still see that mad, smiling face and hear those awful words . . .

ALEX — IT WAS HORRIBLE. SHE WANTED TO HURT ME . . .

IT'S ALL RIGHT, LOVE — SHE'S GONE, FOR GOOD

But even as I said the words, suddenly, I wasn't sure . . .

REMEMBER, ALEX — I'LL NEVER LET YOU GO. NEVER . . . NEVER . . .

NATIONWIDE TALENT HUNT
SWANSEA

WE'LL FIND HIM— BRITAIN'S MOST GORGEOUS GUY!
THIS WEEK:

HAVING A WALES OF A TIME!

Yup! Despite public opinion we've let Julie out again! Over mountains, over vales, now she's ended up in Wales! (Well, Swansea actually.)

★★

★ TALENT SCOUTING ★

Swansea hunting spots:
Valbonne: Trendy — but nice. Temperatures rise in the Tropical room — especially in the corners. ★★★★
Top Rank: (They're everywhere!) Lots of all-boy choir members getting extra practice in with the orchestra. ★★★
Penthouse: Sounds posher than it is. Good place to pick up boys — but put them down quick — you never know where they've been! ★★★

★ PRESENTATION ★

Italy's got the Mafia. Wales has got the Tafia. You can spot them a mile off. Short fat and stocky — if you find one over 5' 2" he's an impostor! But their dark good looks and long eyelashes make up for their platform shoes.

Most of them are steelworkers or miners, so if you hear them talking about slag heaps, they don't necessarily mean you!! ★★★

★ CONTENT ★

All fancy themselves as singers — so lots of moonlight serenades.
Very good at tackles — it's all the rugby practice they put in! Tom Jones impersonations a speciality! Ignore the ones who do Mary Hopkins. ★★★★

Welsh pick-up lines:
"Ever been down a mine?"
"Wanna date with a Welsh Rarebit?"
"Never let a Dai go by!" ★★★

★ STAR QUALITY ★

Welsh boyos are full of chat but very sincere! And they don't try to keep up with the Jones'. Probably 'cos they are the Jones'. ★★★★

★★★★★ *Unforgettable*
★★★★ *Good for a cuddle!*
★★★ *Mmm, not bad!*
★★ *Bad!*
★ *Even badder!*
Forget it!

★ MOST PROMISING NEWCOMER ★

Name: *Dai Jones*
Age: *17*
*Special qualities: Great little mover, especially in a scrum. (Rugby — that is.) Never takes off Tom Jones **or** Harry Secombe. Taller than average (he's 5' 3"). Only wears platform shoes when he tries to kiss you — and who'd look at his feet!*

MYSTERIES OF THE MALE MIND No. 10

Any info you need that you can't live without? Send your questions to Bob! This week: **WHY DO FELLAS ALWAYS WANT TO MEET YOU INSIDE?**

Contrary to public opinion — it's not 'cos we're mean. Nope — it's chivalry . . .

— See you in Tramps about ten. Save you hanging about outside! —

And, when you are inside, you don't want to hang around drinking with us boys, do you??

— Mine's a pint, Bert! Have a nice chat with your mates, luv . . . —

And, if you're not stuck with a fella, you can leave when *you* want . . .

—Time to go luv —bar's shut —

And make your way safely home!

— Lovely night, no point getting a taxi — we'll walk . . .

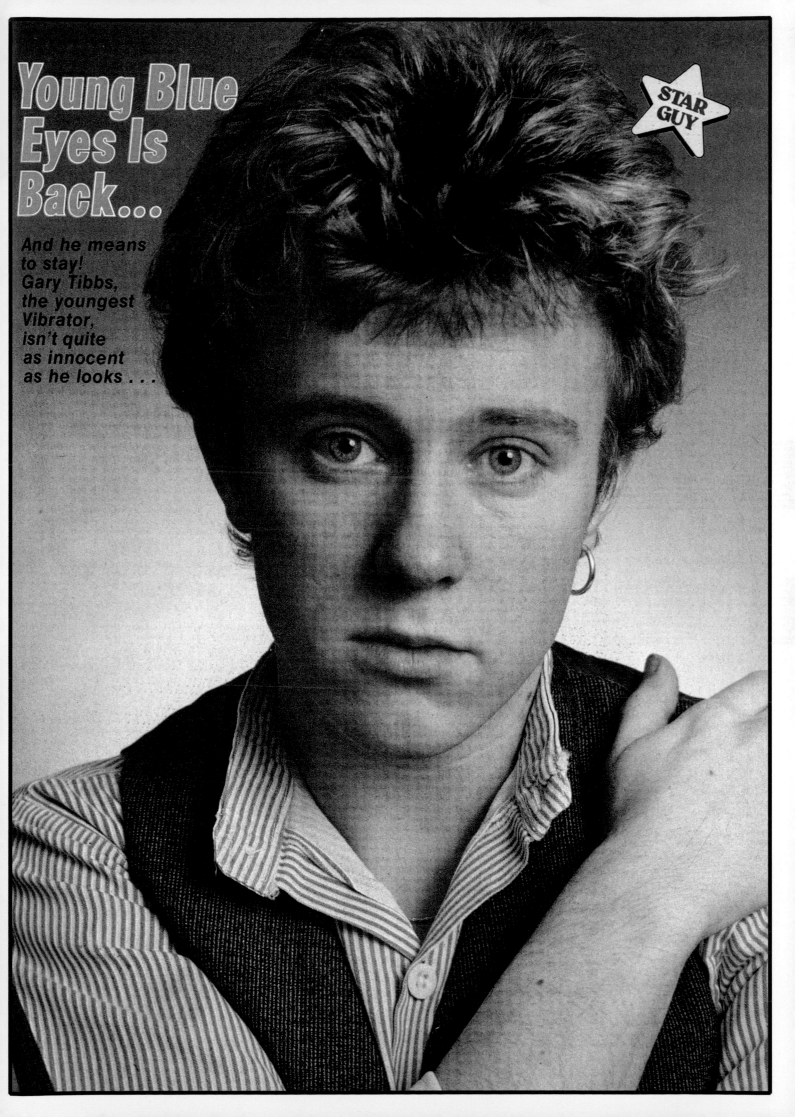

Young Blue Eyes Is Back...

And he means to stay! Gary Tibbs, the youngest Vibrator, isn't quite as innocent as he looks . . .

STAR GUY

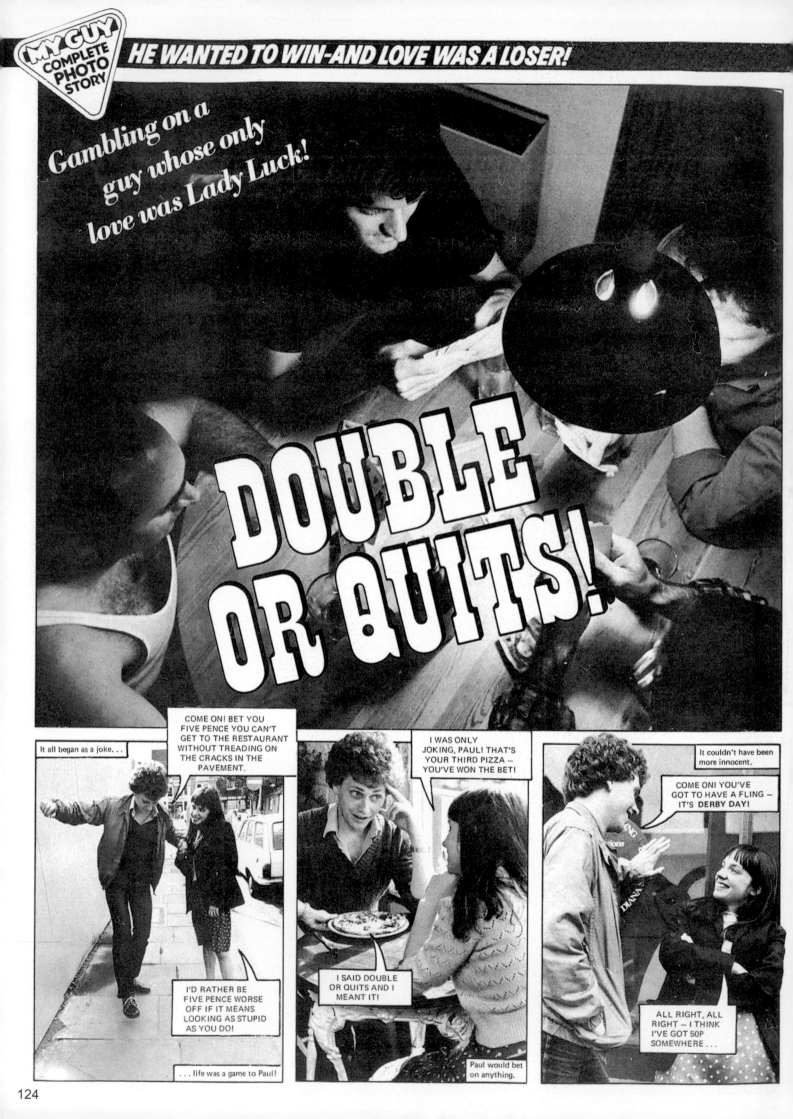

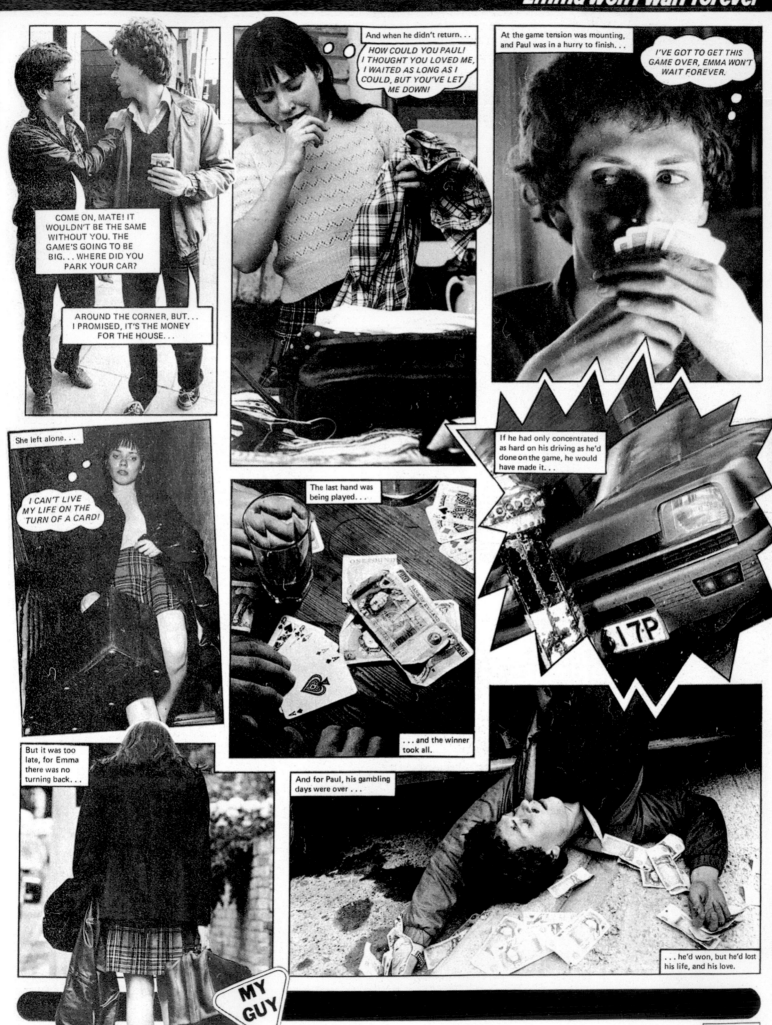

COME ON, MATE! IT WOULDN'T BE THE SAME WITHOUT YOU. THE GAME'S GOING TO BE BIG... WHERE DID YOU PARK YOUR CAR?

AROUND THE CORNER, BUT... I PROMISED, IT'S THE MONEY FOR THE HOUSE...

And when he didn't return...

HOW COULD YOU PAUL! I THOUGHT YOU LOVED ME, I WAITED AS LONG AS I COULD, BUT YOU'VE LET ME DOWN!

At the game tension was mounting, and Paul was in a hurry to finish...

I'VE GOT TO GET THIS GAME OVER, EMMA WON'T WAIT FOREVER.

She left alone...

I CAN'T LIVE MY LIFE ON THE TURN OF A CARD!

The last hand was being played....

...and the winner took all.

If he had only concentrated as hard on his driving as he'd done on the game, he would have made it...

But it was too late, for Emma there was no turning back...

And for Paul, his gambling days were over...

...he'd won, but he'd lost his life, and his love.

MY GUY

THE END

128

MAKE THE BEST OF YOUR CHEST!

Slap one of these smashing shirts on it and no guy'll pass you by! But make sure you nab the right kind of fella — check your top rating here — it could save you a lot of trouble up front!

HE CAN'T RESIST YOU! How could he when you've got 'I Always Get My Guy' written across your chest! In fact, how can *you* resist our amazing t-shirt offer? See below for more details!

MISS ROMANTIC — if you stopped waiting for that knight in shining armour the fellas'd be queuing up! (Cami top from Top Shop £7.99).

GREAT FOR A GIGGLE WITH THE GUYS! No pulling trouble for this type — fellas love you! (Printed top from a selection by Sunarama £2.99)

Our great t-shirt is just £1.99 (p&p included for all sizes!) It's made of 100% cotton which means it's a winner for washing and ironing and comes in red only (the lettering in navy and yellow) with neat cap sleeves. There are three sizes: SMALL — to fit bust 28"/30"; MEDIUM — bust 32"/34" and LARGE — bust 36"/38". To order just fill in *both* coupons below and send with a crossed cheque or postal order (name and address on back of cheque please) made payable to IPC Magazines Ltd. Allow 28 days for delivery, you'll be notified if a longer delay is expected.
NOTE: This offer is only open to readers in England, Scotland, Wales, N. Ireland and Channel Islands. It is not available in Eire or overseas.

SMALL (Bust 28"/30")
MEDIUM (Bust 32"/34")
LARGE (Bust 36"/38")

ALL SIZES
£1.99
including p.&p.

Please send me the T-Shirt(s) as indicated below
I enclose P.O./Cheque No. .... Value..........

No. Required	SMALL	LARGE	MED

NAME: ....
ADDRESS: ....
....
....
Tel. No. (Home or Work) ....

No. Required	SMALL	LARGE	MED

Name: ....
Address: ....
....
....

ANDY'S TYPE — cute and cuddly! You'd rather snuggle up in front of the box than go out on the town! (Top from Top Shop — £5.50).

OOH THE TOUGH TYPE! You know what you want and you always get it! Definitely the local hero's type of girl. (T-shirt by Via Via £5.50).

Showing Tonight!

LATE NIGHT FRILLERS!

Fancy yourself as a real friller? Then get into our naughty nighties and show 'em your star potential!! They won't want their money back . . . !

Left: Get 'em reeling in the stalls with this snuggly butter-wouldn't-melt-in-your-mouth flouncy pink nightie! Credits: From Marks & Spencer, £4.99.
Right: Flash a thigh and they'll be queueing for an encore in this sexy romper suit! Elasticated neckline to wear on or off (!!!) the shoulders. Credits: £3.99 from Dorothy Perkins.
On the table: Guest performances from a cheeky pink nightie, £3.99 from British Home Stores.
And make sure they're outside the box office tomorrow night by being a baby face in this cute baby-doll set in cotton and broderie anglais! £12.50 by Kayser, from most department stores.
Star Wars soap and bubble bath by Cliro, both at 49p, from most chemists.

SHAPE IT AN' FAKE IT!

Not satisfied with your face? Reckon it's less than perfect? Don't think about plastic surgery — just get yourself a good blusher instead! It's cheaper, more fun an' with some good shaping you can give yourself the kinda face you always wanted!

1. Chubby chops? Use a dark blusher under the cheekbone. Try Boots 17 Pearly Shiner for instant highlight!

2. Use a cream blusher to cuten up your nose! Stroke it down the sides and under the tip for a new, slim-line look!

3. Brighten up your bosom! Deepen that cleavage with a dab of Boots 17 Rosy Pearl!

YOU MUST REMEMBER YOUR HIGHNESS, YOU'RE HERE REPRESENTING YOUR COUNTRY, AND YOU CAN'T LET YOUR COUNTRY DOWN.

IF YOU'RE TRYING TO MAKE ME FEEL GUILTY, I DON'T.

But it seemed fate was on her side when the cab collided with another car. . .

YOU STUPID. . .

They were all unharmed. . .

NO PARKING
WE ACCEPT NO LIABILITY FOR DAMAGE TO ANY VEHICLES PARKED HERE

THIS IS VERY UNFORTUNATE, BUT IF YOU DON'T MIND WE'LL PAY YOU AND BE ON OUR WAY. . .

YOU'RE NOT GOING ANYWHERE MATE, I NEED YOU AS A WITNESS! JUST LOOK AT MY CAB!

While Fritz argued with the cab driver, Valeska took the opportunity to slip away. . .

. . .LOOK, YOU DON'T UNDERSTAND, WE'VE GOT TO GO. . .WE'RE DINING WITH LORD BALFONT.

I DON'T CARE IF YOU'RE HAVING LUNCH WITH THE QUEEN, YOU'RE NOT GOING ANYWHERE!

Valeska jumped in the first car she saw. . .

HEY, WHAT'S GOING ON!

HELLO, CAN YOU GIVE ME A LIFT?

WHERE TO?

WHEREVER YOU'RE GOING — BUT QUICK, I'M BEING FOLLOWED!

When Fritz realised she'd gone. . .

OH MY GOD!

HERE, WHERE D'YOU THINK YOU'RE GOING?

WHAT'S SO FUNNY?

WELL I'VE NEVER DONE ANYTHING LIKE THIS BEFORE.

ARE YOU REALLY BEING FOLLOWED, OR ARE YOU KIDDING ME?

NO, I'M SERIOUS.

BLIMEY, IN THAT CASE I NEED A DRINK!

IF HE CAN'T GIVE YOU LOVE...

Having a guy doesn't mean you've found love. Maybe he can't give it to you and you're hanging on to him for something else. Find out here . . .

IS IT YOU . . . ?

1. Do you prefer having lots of other people around to being alone with him? Yes/No

2. Do you like him to spend lots of money on you? Yes/No

3. Are you frightened that you wouldn't get another boyfriend if you chucked him? Yes/No

4. If you knew that doing something would hurt his feelings, would you still go ahead and do it? Yes/No

5. Do you like having a steady fella to show off to your mates? Yes/No

6. Do you ever tease him or upset him on purpose? Yes/No

7. Are you more confident since you've been going out with him? Yes/No

8. Does having him around all the time make you more attractive to other guys? Yes/No

9. Do his compliments boost your ego? Yes/No

10. D'you think you've been going steady too long to start playing the field again now? Yes/No

11. Do you hate talking seriously about your relationship with him? Yes/No

12. Do you feel safe with him 'cos you always know exactly how he'll react to any situation? Yes/No

13. Do you think you've got him under your thumb? Yes/No

14. Do you ever wish you were free, but still feel that you can't chuck him? Yes/No

. . . OR HIM?

15. Does he ever say loving romantic things to you? Yes/No

16. Does he put you before everything else in his life? Yes/No

17. Has he ever said that you're his ideal girl? Yes/No

18. Does he always ask you what you want to do and where you want to go? Yes/No

19. Does he find it easy to forgive you if you've hurt him? Yes/No

20. Is he always keen to see you? Yes/No

21. Does he really care about making you happy? Yes/No

22. Does he think girls are as important as guys? Yes/No

23. Could you ever make him cry? Yes/No

24. Does he admit his faults and mistakes to you? Yes/No

25. D'you think he'd be lost without you? Yes/No

26. Does he make you feel wanted? Yes/No

27. Is he the sort who never takes his bad moods out on you? Yes/No

28. Would he be considerate and comforting if he knew you were feeling down? Yes/No

29. Is he always reliable about turning up on time? Yes/No

30. Does he ever make you feel you're someone special? Yes/No

...WHY DO YOU WANT HIM?

IS IT YOU?

If you answered **mainly 'Yes'** he can't give you love — 'cos you won't let him!

You just aren't interested in having his love — but you do want him for all the other things you get out of him.

You like his money, his attentions and most of all the security he gives you. On top of that you just like the idea of him as a status symbol, a steady fella to impress your mates and even other guys!

But listen — any girl can get those things from almost any guy. Only most girls don't 'cos it isn't specially nice to the guy. And it isn't as satisfying in the long run as having a guy who really loves you, and more important, a guy you can give *your* love to!

Mostly 'No': He can and does give you lots of love. If he didn't you probably wouldn't want to know him!

You're the sort who still believes in romance. You like a guy to feel for you, and you like to feel for him too.

You see guys as people with emotions like your own, that can be hurt. Not just as objects to be used.

And so, in the end, you'll get a lot more out of your guy, than someone who doesn't think like that. You'll get real love — and that can't be beat!

. . . OR HIM?

Mostly 'Yes' and you get plenty of love from your guy — if you want it.

He's tender and loving. He always puts you first, and considers your happiness in everything he does.

Whether you appreciate all this depends on you. If you are the sort who uses guys then he's going to get hurt. But you'd be a fool to reject this one's love.

Take it from us — there aren't many like him around!

Mostly 'No': Better watch out with this guy — 'cos he doesn't care what happens to you. He won't think twice about hurting you or making you unhappy. And he'll be off like a shot if someone he fancies more comes along.

This guy can *love*. It's the ruling passion of his life. But the object of it is . . . himself!

He puts himself, his desires, his feelings, first each and every time. The only look of love he'll give is at the mirror.

If you're just after a steady fella and a good time, he may do for the time being.

But if love is what you're looking for, tell him he doesn't need you, and find someone who does!

MY GUY

ANDY GIBB

We'll go *Shadow Dancing* with him any time! But when are you coming over to show us the real thing, Andy?

MY GUY
CHAPTER FOUR

OUT OF THE DARKNESS

Carol let in a stranger -now she would find the cost of her mistake

I WONDER WHY HE WANTS THE PHONE OFF THE HOOK? HE'S ACT-ING VERY STRANGELY.

I'LL PAY HIS CALL—OUT FEE AND GET RID OF HIM.

EXCUSE ME A MOMENT.

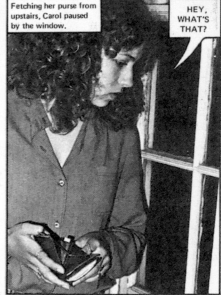

Fetching her purse from upstairs, Carol paused by the window.

HEY, WHAT'S THAT?

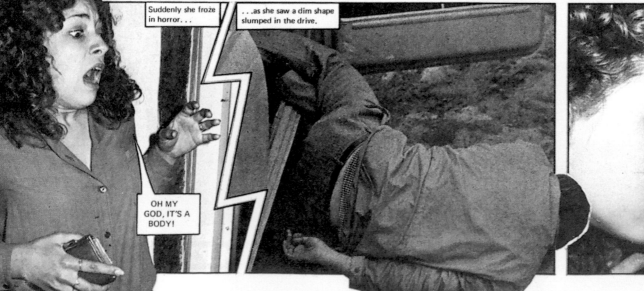

Suddenly she froze in horror. . .

. . .as she saw a dim shape slumped in the drive.

OH MY GOD, IT'S A BODY!

THAT'S THE ELECTRICITY BOARD VAN

YOU & YOUR BODY

If you're worried about *anything* to do with you and your body, then remember, I'm here to help. Write to me, Chris, at: My Guy, 21st Floor, King's Reach Tower, Stamford St., London SE1 9LS.

IS IT SAFE?
I was going to have my ears pierced until I heard that the 'gun' thing they use is dangerous. Is it really?
L. B., Kent.

As long as you have your ears pierced by an experienced jeweller, there is no danger in the use of the 'gun'.

Afterwards, dab a little antiseptic cream on the sleepers and turn them frequently with clean hands until the area is healed.

DAMAGED MYSELF?
I used to masturbate when I was younger and now the lips around my vagina are very swollen and stick out.

I'm worried I'll never be able to have sex properly.
P. K., Cleethorpes.

You've no need to worry as masturbation does not affect the body in any way. These lips, or labia, around your vagina are a normal part of your body.

They develop as your body matures, and are bigger in some girls than in others. Don't think that because of this normal development of your body you will not be able to have sex.

IT'S MUCH BIGGER
One of my breasts is much bigger than the other. I look really lop-sided. Will I always be like this? Is there any exercise that'll help?
Janie A., London.

It's quite common for girls to have one breast bigger than the other, just as one foot is usually bigger than the other!

Exercises are not likely to help, but you may find that as you grow your breasts become more even. Wear a good supporting bra, and don't worry, other people probably don't even notice.

AM I A WOMAN?
I've started my periods but my friend says you're not a proper woman until you have something called ovulation. Please can you tell me what this is?

L. S., Powys.

Ovulation is the release of an egg from an ovary. It happens about once a month, usually two weeks before a period.

What your friend means is that a girl is not fertile unless her body releases an egg in preparation for conceiving a baby.

Most girls ovulate when they first get their periods. It is possible to have periods without ovulation taking place, usually at the start of your periods when they are still irregular.

NASTY KNICKERS
I sometimes get a rash all round my vagina and at the tops of my thighs. Could wearing nylon knickers cause this? Or might it be the soap powder I wash them in?
F. R., Essex.

Nylon certainly aggravates a sensitive skin. Try wearing cotton knickers or ones with a cotton-lined gusset. Avoid tight jeans as they can often

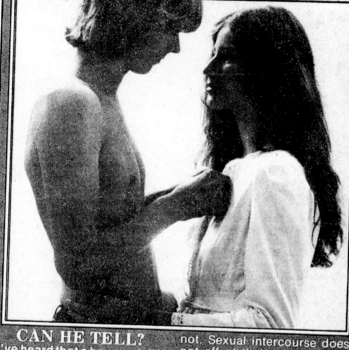

CAN HE TELL?
I've heard that a boy can tell if you're a virgin by the size of your breasts. They get bigger when you get your periods and having sex makes them grow too. I've got quite large breasts and I don't want my boyfriend to think I'm not a virgin.

D. W., Worcester.

You've been listening to an old wives' tale. The size of your breasts has nothing to do with whether you're a virgin or not. Sexual intercourse does not affect their size or bring about any other outward physical changes in you. Having a large bust does not mean that other people will think you're not a virgin.

Getting your periods isn't a magical sign for your bust to develop either. They are both part of the bodily changes that take place when you go through puberty, your bust can develop before, or some times after you get your periods.

cause irritation. Be very careful about general hygiene too.

Use a mild soap powder such as Lux to wash your undies. Many people are sensitive to biological powders if all traces of soap are not washed out.

LOOKING GOOD!

Any special beauty problems? I'll sort them out and keep you looking great!

BRUSH OFF
I'm really useless at applying make-up, I always end up with half of it on my hands and the other half somewhere else!
Carol, Banbury.

It's time to get yourself organised! Save your make-up for your face by using the right applicators — Boots do a good selection of make-up brushes.

Try the Complexion Brush (35p), you'll find your blusher will go on twice as smoothly. For applying powder eyeshadow, instead of your fingers use the soft wedge-shaped brush (45p). There's also a 3 in 1 brush with a sponge applicator (85p), useful for cream shadow or

blending colours. After you've mascared your lashes use the Eyelash Brush (20p) for separating the lashes.

TOUCH OF COLOUR
My hair looks so drab and dull. How can I brighten it up?
Elly, Blackpool.

Try Boots new Sure & Simple shampoo in Permanent Hair Colour. There are ten shades to choose from, to lighten, darken or just brighten up your natural hair colour.

Each pack contains a tube of colourant, a bottle of developer and a pair of plastic gloves. All you do is mix the two ingredients, following

the instructions, and use as you would a shampoo. Sure & Simple costs 59p, from branches of Boots.

BROW BEATEN
I shaved my eyebrows 'cos they were really bushy. Now they've grown back worse than ever!
Lindy, Horsham.

For starters, never shave your eyebrows! You'll spoil their natural shape.

Use tweezers to pluck your brows and always pluck hairs from underneath and in the direction the hair grows. If you find it painful, soak a pad of cotton wool in warm water and hold it against your skin. This will open the pores and make plucking easier. Use an antiseptic cream like Savlon afterwards to prevent infection. Once you've got your eyebrows into shape, you'll find you only need to pluck out stray hairs every day or so.

THE HELP PAGES

I'M STILL A VIRGIN!

I'm the only girl I know who's still a virgin. I always feel the odd one out when I'm with my mates. Most of them are on the Pill and have had sex. They treat me like a kid and say I don't know what I'm missing.

I haven't got a steady boyfriend but there's one guy who's always been keen on me. I want to stop feeling so left out and I think I'd quite like to sleep with him. Do you think I should?

J. F., Gainsborough.

Doing things you don't want to just to keep up with others is never a good idea. And it's downright silly when it's something as serious as losing your virginity. Sex is not something to be entered into lightly.

You'd just be using this boy which, as you don't feel very strongly about him, wouldn't be fair to either of you. Casual sex, without a stable, loving relationship, will leave you feeling hurt and used.

And, if the truth be known, your mates are probably not so experienced as they make out. They're just trying to impress you. Ignore their remarks and don't do anything you'd regret.

HE WON'T SPEAK TO ME

I met my brother's best mate, Jim, when I was out shopping last week and he asked me to go for a coffee. I was dead chuffed when he asked to see me again. When my brother found out, he went mad and told me to find my own friends instead of pinching his. Now he won't speak to me and I don't know what to do.

Lesley P., Falmouth.

Your brother doesn't appreciate that you're not his little sister any more. He just hasn't realised that you're ready to date fellas and it's a shock to him to find that his best mate finds you attractive!

He's jealous as well, as he probably feels he's losing Jim's friendship to you. Reassure him, 'cos even if he does make things awkward for a while, he'll come round once he realises you and Jim are serious about each other.

ON THE SHELF?

I can't get a boyfriend. All my mates are going out with steady fellas, I'm the only one who never goes out with anyone. I always try to look attractive and be interested in the boys I meet but it doesn't seem to do any good. What's wrong with me?

P. K., Kettering.

Nothing. But maybe you're making too much of an effort and that's what's putting the fellas off. You're starting to feel desperate and it shows!

Guys don't like to feel they're being pushed into anything, especially by a girl. So stop worrying, play it a bit cooler and they'll soon come running.

HE'S CHANGED

I'm still at school, studying for A-levels. Rob, my boyfriend, left to work in a garage.

He never talks to me much now and I think it's because I'm cleverer than he is. I don't want to lose him as he's nice and really good-looking but he's no fun any more. What shall I do?

Maggie L., Lincs.

Are you sure it's all his fault? Just because he works in a garage doesn't mean he's got no brains or feelings. Maybe he's not talking to you because he feels you wouldn't listen anyway.

If you want to stay with Rob, stop feeling so superior and start caring.

I HAVE TO SAY SORRY

My boyfriend and I have been arguing a lot lately but it's always me who ends up saying sorry — even when I know the row hasn't been my fault. I'm beginning to think

IT'S NOTHING TO WORRY ABOUT...

PARTIES

The one place you should enjoy yourself is at a party. But sometimes you can find yourself missing out on all the fun . . .

What do I do if I end up with no-one to speak to?
If you can't see anyone you know, ask the person who invited you to introduce you to a few other people. If he/she's not around then don't wait for others to come to you. Get in on the party atmosphere and introduce yourself. Something like 'Hi, my name's . . . do you live round here?' will soon get you talking.

Should you get really tarted up?
A party's a special occasion so naturally everyone makes an effort to look good. Don't be outdone, make the most of yourself. But even though your looks may be the first thing to catch a fella's eye, it's your personality he's really interested in. So look good but concentrate on being good company 'cos that's what counts!

What do you do if you get landed with a creep?
Make an excuse to dance with someone else, disappear to the loo for a good ten minutes or say you must go and talk to your mate who's on the other side of the room. He'll soon get the message and leave you alone.

Is it safe to go to a party when there are no parents around?
Yes, so long as the parents of whoever is giving the party know that it's taking place.

Just because there's nobody watching over you doesn't mean it'll turn into an orgy! There's no need to go wild either. Be sensible and enjoy yourself. If you feel things are getting out of hand then leave.

What should I do if everyone's drinking?
Don't worry about them, keep a clear head and stick to soft drinks, you'll enjoy yourself just as much. If you drink alcohol, you may do something you'd regret or find yourself in an embarrassing situation with a boy.

Should I go upstairs with a boy?
You could be letting yourself in for a lot more than you'd bargained for if you do. It's easy to get carried away at a party, everyone's happy and enjoying themselves. But don't let yourself go too far. Stay with the rest of the party and keep on safe ground.

Should I arrange for a lift home?
It's the first thing you should do once you know you're going to a party.

It's no good trusting to luck, there's nothing worse than being stranded miles from home or having to fork out for a taxi! And it's certainly not fair to make your parents worry. So check on the times of last buses etc. or fix up a lift with a reliable person. You'll enjoy the evening more if you've no worries about getting home.

GOT PROBLEMS...

Depressed? Worried about something? Then you need some-one to talk to. And that's just what I'm here for! Write and tell me what's bothering you and I'll do my best to help. I'm Chris and the address is: My Guy, 21st Floor, King's Reach Tower, Stamford Street, London SE1 9LS.

RAT OF THE WEEK!

If he's a Rat, he'll use you, then leave you heartbroken, as this reader found out.

I was all alone while my mum was in hospital, my dad's been dead for quite a few years now.

I felt really lonely and depre-ssed until I met this wonderful fella. It seemed he'd really fal-len for me.

He was living in a crummy bed-sit, so I started cooking meals for him and doing his washing. I'd have done any-thing for him 'cos I thought he loved me.

Then my mum came home and that was it. He dropped me flat! 'Cos now he didn't have free meals and a laundry service. He'd just been using me all along.

If you know someone who's a Rat, write and let me know, marking the envelope 'Rat of the Week'.

---

he likes rowing just for the sake of it.
Pippa, Cleethorpes.

Always giving in to someone means you run the risk of being walked over. You're under his thumb if it's always you that apologises. And, quite naturally, he doesn't respect you for it.

Next time an argument starts, stick to your point of view and don't give in. If he's genuinely fond of you he'll have to come round in the end.

HE'S DISGUSTING!
I love being with my boy-friend only he's got one awful habit. Whenever he's driving anywhere, he always whis-tles and yells something at any girl he sees. He even winks at other girls when I'm with him. What can I do?
Teresa, Stockport.

I don't think you've got too much to worry about so long as you're the girl who matters most to him. Do your best to laugh about it — you'll only encourage him if he thinks he's making you jealous.

HE WON'T STOP!
How can I get my boyfriend to stop giving me lovebites? My neck gets covered in bruises and I have to wear polo necks and scarves to hide them.
Mandy, King's Lynn.

Explain to him that you'd rather be kissed properly than end up with a bruised neck. Every time you feel he's hom-ing in for a quick nibble, turn it into a kiss instead.

---

start fancying *her* and ignor-ing me.
I lost my last boyfriend arguing about this. Please help.
S. D., Watford.

Your self-confidence has taken a knock over losing your last boyfriend but are you sure you're not blaming your mum unfairly? Perhaps you and your boyfriend would have broken up anyway.

Have more faith in yourself. After all, you're the one that's being asked out, not your mum. Just feel proud that your fellas like her and don't think of her as competition!

BAD REPUTATION
At a disco I met this fella. We had a great evening together and I didn't let him go further than putting his arm round me. But next day I heard some other boys say-ing he was only after what he could get.
Should I see him again?
Penny L., Middlesbrough.

And if he still doesn't take the hint, take to wearing your polo neck jumpers when you're out with him — he won't enjoy a mouthful of wool!

THEY FANCY HER
My mum is very young-looking. A lot of people think she's my older sister. I don't mind that except when I take boyfriends home and they

---

You'd be stupid to let idle gossip influence your feelings about this boy. The only way you can find out what he's really like is from your own feelings about him and the way he treats you. It's very unfair to listen to other people and form your opinion of him from what they say.

HE SCARES ME
This friend of my dad's has been coming to see us ever since I was little. Recently though he's changed towards me, he seems to like touching me and is always putting his hand on my knee. I'm scared to be left alone with him now.
E. K., Cambridge.

You must make it very clear to this man that you don't like him touching you. Always make sure there's someone else with you when he comes round and, if it happens again, tell your parents straight away – they'll want to help.

GUYS – I'LL HELP YOU TOO!

SHE TURNS ME ON!
One of my mother's friends is really attractive, she looks about 18! I'm sure she fancies me — she's always chatting to me now and putting her arm round me.
What makes it worse is I know her son very well, he's just joined the Merchant Navy. What d'you think I should do?
Pete D., Yorks.

You're letting your imagina-tion run away with you. This woman obviously likes you but it's my guess she's probably missing her son and you're fil-ling the gap left by him.
Stay friendly with her but don't get the wrong idea. Con-centrate on girls of your own age instead.

HOW CAN I STOP HER?
My girlfriend didn't mind me smoking at first. Now she keeps on about me ruining my health and what a waste of money smoking is. Her nag-ging's getting me down.
Rob D., Surrey.

She's got a good point, you know, smoking really is bad for your health and expensive! Why not compromise. Cut down on the fags, especially when you're with her. Once she sees you're making an effort to stop for her sake, she should stop her nagging and start encouraging you instead.

NO SEX
I've been going with my girl for about a year now. She says she loves me but I can't understand why she won't sleep with me. I've told her I'd be careful but that doesn't seem to be enough. What's wrong with her?
Shaun M., Liverpool.

Nothing. But the way you're treating her is all wrong. It's not just a fear of pregnancy that's stopping her. She obviously realises that sex is more than physical, it's emotional too.
It seems that for you the phys-ical side of things is everything. With that attitude you're not ready to cope with a sexual rela-tionship. Forget sex for now,

---

and concentrate on being more sensitive and building up a good emotional relationship with your girl.

BABY SNATCHER
Do you think there's any-thing wrong in a bloke my age, 18, going out with a girl of 13?
My mates have found out and keep saying I've raided the cradle.
Robbie L., Andover

Don't listen to your mates — as long as you're both happy, that's all that counts. But five years is a big gap, and she may not want to go steady at the age of 13. Keep it fairly casual.

MY GUY
PETER POWELL

Radio 1's tastiest
dee-jay — tune in and
have a treat!

Top left cover:

FESTIVAL OF FREEBIES!

WIN A RADIO CASSETTE RECORDER!

MY GUY

16p

No. 33
EVERY SATURDAY
14th OCTOBER 1978

NEW PHOTO STORY!

STAR GUY

What sort of guy would she get from—
THE LOVE MACHINE

CRAZEE ABOUT HIM!
(Captain Ken, of course!)

PROBLEM STORY
'My guy's not a real man!'

AUSTRALIA 35c. NEW ZEALAND 35c. SOUTH AFRICA 38c. MALAYSIA $1.23

Top right cover:

AMAZING ADAM ANT PIN-UP!

MY GUY

22
No. 1
EVERY SATURDAY 4th JULY 19

COMPLETE PHOTO STORY

ASTRAL BEAUTY Part 3

STAND AND DELIVER
Her secret—or her life!

Find out fate's face for you!

STAR GUY

THE LUCK OF THE IRISH!
How the Moondogs made it overnight

PHOTO PROBLEM
I'm always in fear at parties!

AUSTRALIA 50c. NEW ZEALAND 50c.
MALAYSIA $1.50

Bottom left cover:

NEW! REAL LIFE, REAL LOVE—IN PHOTOS!

MY GUY

14p

EVERY SATURDAY   No. 3 18th MARCH 1978

40 PAGES

FREE!

HAPPY HEART BADGE

HOW DEEP IS THEIR LOVE?

IT COULD BE WORTH
£100
TO YOU!

BOYS JUST SAY 'NO' TO ME!
See how you could lose in love

NEW PHOTO STORY— DON'T PLAY WITH FIRE!

AUSTRALIA 35c. NEW ZEALAND 35c.
SOUTH AFRICA 38c. MALAYSIA $1.23

Bottom right cover:

Grease! READ THE ROCK 'N' ROLL LOVE STORY INSIDE

MY GUY

16p
No. 3
EVERY SATURDAY 18th NOVEMBER 197

NEW PHOTO STORY!

When Tessa's around...
GIRLS MUST BE GUYS!

MUST HE GET UPSET?

STAR GUY

TEMPTING TARGET!
The hunk you love to hate...

PHOTO PROBLEM
SHOULD I BEG FOR HER BOY